Edexcel Award in
Statistical
Methods

Level **2**

WORKBOOK

D1337443

Peter Sherran

ALWAYS LEARNING

PEARSON

Published by Pearson Education Limited, Edinburgh Gate, Harlow, Essex, CM20 2JE.

www.pearsonschoolsandfecolleges.co.uk

Text © Pearson Education Limited 2013
Edited by Project One Publishing Solutions, Scotland
Typeset and illustrated by Tech-Set Ltd, Gateshead
Original illustrations © Pearson Education Limited 2013
Cover image © AXL / Shutterstock.com

The right of Peter Sherran to be identified as author of this work has been asserted by him in accordance with the Copyright, Designs and Patents Act 1988.

First published 2013

17 16 15 14 13
10 9 8 7 6 5 4 3 2 1

British Library Cataloguing in Publication Data
A catalogue record for this book is available from the British Library

ISBN 978 1 446 90330 8

Copyright notice
All rights reserved. No part of this publication may be reproduced in any form or by any means (including photocopying or storing it in any medium by electronic means and whether or not transiently or incidentally to some other use of this publication) without the written permission of the copyright owner, except in accordance with the provisions of the Copyright, Designs and Patents Act 1988 or under the terms of a licence issued by the Copyright Licensing Agency, Saffron House, 6–10 Kirby Street, London EC1N 8TS (www.cla.co.uk). Applications for the copyright owner's written permission should be addressed to the publisher.

Printed in Slovakia by Neografia

Acknowledgements
Every effort has been made to contact copyright holders of material reproduced in this book. Any omissions will be rectified in subsequent printings if notice is given to the publishers.

Disclaimer
This material has been published on behalf of Edexcel and offers high-quality support for the delivery of Edexcel qualifications.

This does not mean that the material is essential to achieve any Edexcel qualification, nor does it mean that it is the only suitable material available to support any Edexcel qualification. Material from this publication will not be used verbatim in any examination or assessment set by Edexcel. Any resource lists produced by Edexcel shall include this and other appropriate resources.

Copies of official specifications for all Edexcel qualifications may be found on the Edexcel website: www.edexcel.com

In the writing of this book, no Edexcel examiners authored sections relevant to examination papers for which they have responsibility.

Notices

The GCSE links provide references to course books as follows:

AF Edexcel GCSE Mathematics A Foundation Student Book
BF Edexcel GCSE Mathematics B Foundation Student Book
16+ Edexcel GCSE Mathematics 16+ Student Book
S Edexcel GCSE Mathematics Statistics

Contents

Self-assessment chart

	Needs more practice	Almost there	I'm proficient!	Notes
Chapter 1 Data				
1.1 Type of data	☐	☐	☐	
1.2 Sampling	☐	☐	☐	
1.3 Design a question for a questionnaire	☐	☐	☐	
1.4 Bias in sampling methods	☐	☐	☐	
1.5 Calculate a stratified sample	☐	☐	☐	
Chapter 2 Displaying data				
2.1 Compose bar charts	☐	☐	☐	
2.2 Two-way tables	☐	☐	☐	
2.3 Time-series graphs	☐	☐	☐	
2.4 Stem and leaf diagrams	☐	☐	☐	
2.5 Grouped frequency tables	☐	☐	☐	
2.6 Frequency polygons	☐	☐	☐	
2.7 Cumulative frequency diagrams	☐	☐	☐	
2.8 Box plots	☐	☐	☐	
2.9 Histograms	☐	☐	☐	
2.10 Sample space diagrams	☐	☐	☐	
2.11 Misleading diagrams	☐	☐	☐	
Chapter 3 Calculating with data				
3.1 Calculating means for grouped and ungrouped data	☐	☐	☐	
3.2 The median and interquartile range	☐	☐	☐	
3.3 Moving averages and fixed-base index numbers	☐	☐	☐	
3.4 Mean and standard deviation	☐	☐	☐	
Chapter 4 Interpreting data				
4.1 Interpret and compare charts and diagrams	☐	☐	☐	
4.2 The modal class interval	☐	☐	☐	
4.3 Class intervals containing the median	☐	☐	☐	
4.4 Outliers	☐	☐	☐	
4.5 Lines of best fit and trend lines	☐	☐	☐	
4.6 Skew	☐	☐	☐	
4.7 Comparing data – interquartile range, skew and standard deviation	☐	☐	☐	
4.8 Making predictions	☐	☐	☐	
4.9 Moving averages and fixed-base index numbers	☐	☐	☐	
Chapter 5 Probability				
5.1 Compare probability and relative frequency	☐	☐	☐	
5.2 Add probabilities	☐	☐	☐	
5.3 Use sample space diagrams to calculate probabilities	☐	☐	☐	
5.4 Use probability to estimate outcomes	☐	☐	☐	
5.5 Multiply probabilities using tree diagrams	☐	☐	☐	

GCSE LINKS

AH: 6.1 Introduction to Statistics;
BF: Unit 11.1 Introduction to Statistics; S: 1.2 Types of data

1.1 Types of data

By the end of this section you will know how to:

※ Recognise and describe different types of data

Key points

※ **Discrete data** can only take specific values.

※ **Continuous data** can take any numerical value in a given range.

※ **Categorical data** is described by words rather than numbers.

1 Here are some examples of data.

A The time taken for a pedestrian to cross a road.

B The height of a Year 9 pupil.

C The number of pages in a book.

D The colour of the ink in a biro.

E The prime numbers less than 100.

F The total of a tally.

G The speed of a train.

Write each of the letters A–G in one of the circles to describe the type of data.

Categorical   Discrete   Continuous

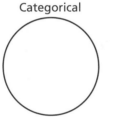 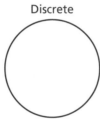 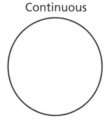

You should know

Measurement of distance, weight, temperature or time gives continuous data.

2 Kate keeps a record of her music collection:

Album names   **Length of the tracks**   **Type of music**

a What type of data are the **Album names**? ....

b What type of data are the **Lengths of the tracks**? ....

c What type of data are the **Types of music**? ....

3 Here is a six-sided spinner. After each spin, Tim records the score and Alex records whether the score is odd or even.

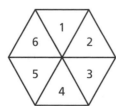

a What type of data does Tim record? ....

b What type of data does Alex record? ....

Step into GCSE

4 Lucy collects data about the different types of fish in her pond.
She measures the length and the weight of each fish.
What are the three types of data that Lucy collects?

Type of fish .... Length ....

Weight ....

5 Paul takes part in a nationwide survey about birds.
He records the types of birds he sees in his garden and how many there are.
Describe the two types of data that Paul collects.

Type of bird ....

Number seen ....

6 Complete the table by ticking the correct box in each row.

Data	Data type		
	Categorical	**Discrete**	**Continuous**
The temperature inside a fridge			
The makes of car in a car park			
The number of people at a cricket match			
The colour of sweets in a jar			
The area of a rectangle			

Needs more practice ☐ Almost there ☐ I'm proficient! ☐

1.2 Sampling

By the end of this section you will know how to:

* Recognise the difference between a sample and a population
* Understand why sampling is used

GCSE LINKS
AH: 6.2 Sampling methods;
BH: Unit 11.2 Sampling methods;
S: 1.6 Populations and sampling

Key points

* A **population** is a complete collection of people, creatures or objects from which data may be collected for an enquiry.
* A **sample** is some part of the population chosen to represent the population.
* In a **census**, data is collected from every member of the population.

1 Toby works at a bakery.
He selects a sample from every batch of loaves produced and checks them for quality.

   a State the population for each quality check.

....

....

> **Hint**
> Each sample is taken from a complete collection of objects.

   b Explain why Toby takes a sample rather than a census.

....

....

....

....

> **Hint**
> Testing a loaf for quality will mean that it can't be sold.

2 Bella wants to know how much time drivers expect to save by using the M6 toll road.
She carries out a survey by asking a sample of drivers as they pass through a toll gate.

   a State the population for the survey.

....

....

> **Hint**
> The population is made up of everyone relevant to the survey.

   b Explain why Bella takes a sample rather than a census.

....

....

....

....

> **Hint**
> Think about trying to ask everyone in the population.

3 A television ratings company in the UK surveys a sample audience to work out which television programmes are the most popular.

   a Describe the population for this survey.

....

   b Explain why a sample is taken rather than a census.

....

....

....

4 An examiner may mark around 500 exam papers. A lead examiner will select a sample of these papers and re-mark them to check that the papers have been marked consistently.

   a State the population for the checking process.

....

   b Explain why a sample is taken rather than a census.

....

....

....

1.3 Design a question for a questionnaire

By the end of this section you will know how to:

✳ Design a question for a questionnaire

GCSE LINKS

AH: 6.5 Questionnaires;
BH: Unit 11.5 Questionnaires;
16+: 19.2 Design and criticise questions for questionnaires;
S: 1.9 Collecting data

Key points

✳ Each question of a **questionnaire** is designed to collect data for a particular purpose.

✳ Avoid wording that suggests a particular response as this makes the question **biased**.

✳ Make each question clear and easily understood.

✳ Do not include questions that may embarrass the person being asked.

✳ Allow for the full range of responses.

✳ Do not ask questions that are too difficult.

Guided

1 Here are some questions that are not suitable for a questionnaire. For each one, give a reason why the question is unsuitable.

> **Remember this**
> There should be no hint of what the expected answer is.

a The people of this town do not want a new supermarket. Do you agree?

☐ Yes ☐ No ☐ Undecided

....

....

b How much do you earn in a week?

☐ More than £600 ☐ £500–£600
☐ £400–£499 ☐ Less than £400

> **Hint**
> Some people may have very little money to spend on new clothes.

....

....

c How often do you travel by train?

☐ All the time ☐ Quite often
☐ Sometimes ☐ Not very often

> **Hint**
> Are you clear about the choices? What do they mean?

....

....

d How many films do you watch in a month?

☐ 0–5 ☐ 5–10
☐ 10–15 ☐ More than 15

> **Hint**
> Is it always clear which box to tick?

....

....

2 Rewrite each of the following questions to make them suitable for a questionnaire.

a Do you agree that students should be able to use the computer room at lunchtime?

☐ Yes   ☐ No   ☐ Don't know

Do you agree or .... that students should be able to use the computer room at lunchtime?

☐ Agree   ☐ ....   ☐ Don't know

b Which of these meals is your favourite?

☐ Salad   ☐ Fish and chips   ☐ A pasta dish   ☐ Curry

Which of these meals is your favourite?

☐ Salad   ☐ Fish and chips   ☐ A pasta dish   ☐ Curry   ☐ .... of these

c How much time do you usually spend on homework in a week?

☐ 0–3 hours   ☐ 3–6 hours   ☐ 6–9 hours

How much time do you usually spend on homework in a week?

☐ 0–3 hours   ☐ 4–6 hours   ☐ .... hours   ☐ More than .... hours

d Do you think that revision guides are helpful?

☐ Yes   ☐ No

Do you think that revision guides are helpful?

☐ Yes   ☐ No   ☐ ....

3 Say what you think is wrong with these questionnaire questions.
Rewrite them to make them more suitable.

a How many times a week do you eat bread?

☐ Less than 5   ☐ 5 or 6   ☐ 6 or 7   ☐ More than 7

....
....
....
....

b How many footsteps do you take on average per day?

☐ Less than 1800   ☐ 1800 – 1999   ☐ 2000 – 2200   ☐ More than 2200

....
....
....
....

c Do you agree that eating too many crisps will make you gain weight?

  ☐ Yes   ☐ No   ☐ Don't know

....

....

....

....

4 A group of women are given a sample of face cream to try and are then asked to complete a questionnaire. Here is one of the questions:

How do you rate this product?

  ☐ Excellent

  ☐ Very good

  ☐ Good

a Explain why the original question was biased.

....

....

....

b Rewrite the question so that it is not biased.

....

....

....

....

....

....

....

5 A company sells goods directly to customers over the internet.
The manager wants to know how satisfied the customers are with the quality of service.
Design a suitable question for a questionnaire.

....

....

....

....

....

....

....

Step into GCSE

1.4 Bias in sampling methods

GCSE LINKS
AH: 6.7 Sources of bias;
BH: Unit 11.7 Sources of bias;
S: 1.7 Random sampling

By the end of this section you will know how to:

* Identify sources of bias in sampling methods
* Recognise when the results from a sample will not be reliable

Key points

* A sample is **biased** if it does not represent the population.
* A sample which is **too small** to represent the population may be biased.
* A **random sample** is one in which every member of the population has an equal chance of being selected.
* Using a random sample is one way to avoid bias.
* Choosing a sample that is biased will produce results that are not **reliable**.

1 A town council carries out a survey to find out if people are in favour of increasing the number of times a market is held in the town from once a month to once a week.
The survey is taken on a market day.
Explain why the sample of people chosen is likely to be biased.

> **Hint**
> Do you think the sample chosen will fairly represent the views of the town?

....

....

....

....

....

2 A survey is taken to find out if people feel that all dogs should be muzzled when outdoors.
The people taking part in the survey were walking their dogs in a local park.
Explain why the sample of people chosen is likely to be biased.

> **Hint**
> Is it likely that the sample chosen will fairly represent the views of the general public?

....

....

....

....

....

....

3 A conference for teachers is held on a sunny Saturday. There are talks throughout the day but the teachers attending are free to choose which ones to attend. At the end of the last talk of the day, a questionnaire is handed out to assess the value of the talks. Explain why the sample of people responding to the survey may be biased.

Hint

Think about which people would be there at the end of the day.

....

....

....

....

....

4 A survey was designed to find out if people thought that there were too few facilities for teenagers in the local area. A random sample of people was asked at a shopping centre between 10am and 11am on a Monday morning. Comment on the reliability of the survey.

....

....

....

....

....

5 A reporter for a magazine is writing an article about the types of movie that people most like to see. He asks fifty people leaving a cinema. Explain why the information collected may not be reliable.

....

....

....

....

....

6 A random sample of ten people in a shopping centre is asked for their views on the safety of the equipment at a local playground.

a Give two reasons why the results of the survey may not be reliable.

1 ....

....

2 ....

....

b Describe the changes you would introduce to make the survey more reliable.

....

....

....

1.5 Calculate a stratified sample

By the end of this section you will know how to:

* Calculate a stratified sample so that a group within the population is fairly represented

GCSE LINKS
AH: 6.3 Stratified sampling;
BH: Unit 11.3 Stratified sampling;
S: 1.7 Random sampling

Key points

* The population may be divided into groups, or **strata**, such as males and females.
* A **stratified sample** contains members of every group in proportion to the size of the group.
* The number of members of a group taken as part of a stratified sample is given by

$$\frac{\text{Group size}}{\text{Population size}} \times \text{Sample size}$$

1 There are 35 girls and 25 boys in the school choir.
A stratified sample of 12 students is taken.
Find the number of girls in the sample.

Group size = ...

Population size = 25 + 35 = ...

Number of girls in sample = $\frac{35}{\text{........}}$ × 12 = ...

2 650 people have joined a new gym.
There are 180 full-time members and the rest are part-time members.
A stratified sample of 50 members is taken.
Work out the number of full-time members in the sample.

You should know

Round your answer to the nearest whole number.

3 A company produces coats for dogs. The coats are made in three sizes.
The table gives information about the number of each size made in one day.

Small	Medium	Large
34	85	21

A stratified sample of 20 coats is taken.
Find the number of large coats in the sample.

4 A theatre has three types of seating available.
The table gives information about the numbers of seats used for one performance.

Front stalls	Rear stalls	Circle
196	284	223

A stratified sample of 30 audience members is taken.
Find how many people in the sample had a seat in the Circle.

Don't forget!

✳ Discrete data can only take .... values.

✳ Continuous data can take any .... value in a given ....

✳ Categorical data is described by .... rather than ....

✳ A sample is some part of the population chosen to .... the population.

✳ Each question of a questionnaire is designed to collect data for a particular ....

✳ Avoid wording that suggests a particular response as this makes the question ....

✳ A sample is biased if it does not represent the ....

✳ A random sample is one in which every member of the population has an .... chance of being selected.

✳ The population may be divided into groups, or ...., such as males and females.

✳ A stratified sample contains members of every group in .... to the size of the group.

Exam-style questions

1 Suzy plans to buy a minibus for a school. She records the make and model of each minibus and the number of seats available for passengers.
Complete the table.

Data collected	Data type
Make and model	
Number of passenger seats	

2 Some Year 11 students want to measure the support for the idea that they should always be allowed an early lunch. They decide to use a questionnaire.
Design a suitable question.

....

....

....

....

....

3 Sundeep wants to know how many magazines people read. He asks 10 people in his class.
Give two reasons why Sundeep's sample may be biased.

1 ....

....

2 ....

....

4 The table shows the number of students in each Key Stage at a school.

KS3	KS4	KS5
640	458	162

A stratified sample of 40 students at the school is taken.
Find the number of KS5 students in the sample.

....

Composite bar charts

2.1

By the end of this section you will know how to:

　＊　Draw composite bar charts

GCSE LINKS

AH: 18.4 Interpreting comparative and composite bar charts;

BF: Unit 1 3.4 Interpreting comparati~~ve~~ and composite bar charts;

S: 2.15 Using bar charts to make comparisons

Key points

　＊　The **height** or **length** of each bar shows the **total value represented**.

　＊　Each bar is subdivided into parts representing sub-categories.

　＊　The bars may be horizontal or vertical.

　＊　There should be a gap between the bars.

　＊　The bars should all be the same width.

　＊　The axes on a bar chart should be clearly labelled.

　＊　Use a key to describe what the parts of the bars represent.

Guided

1 The table gives information about the membership of a golf club.

	Juniors	Adults	Seniors
Male	8	38	14
Female	6	24	16

Draw a composite bar chart for this data.

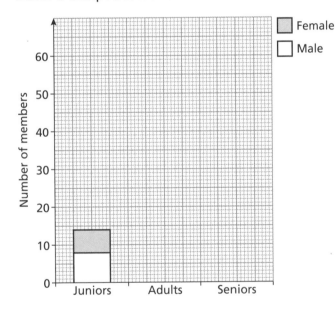

Hint

Work out the total for Adults. Draw a bar of this height and shade the part representing Females. Do the same thing for Seniors.

Practice

2 Two chocolate biscuit bars were compared. The table gives information about the ingredients of the two bars.

	Economy	Finest
Chocolate	5%	15%
Biscuit	80%	80%
Other	15%	5%

Draw a composite bar chart for this data.

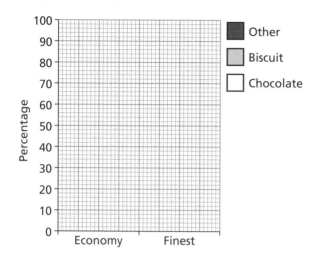

3 The table shows how students from two different schools performed in their GCSE maths exams last year.

		School 1	School 2
Maths GCSE grades	**A*–C**	62%	75%
	D–E	27%	16%
	F–G	11%	9%

Use the information in the table to draw a composite bar chart.

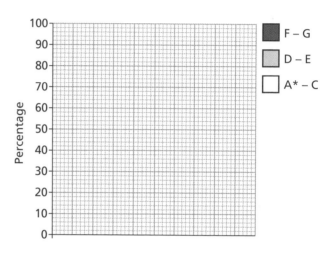

Needs more practice ☐   **Almost there** ☐   **I'm proficient!** ☐

2.2 Two-way tables

By the end of this section you will know how to:

* Draw two-way tables

GCSE LINKS

AH: 6.6 Two-way tables;
BH: Unit 11.6 Two-way and other tables; **16+:** 19.3 Designing and using two-way tables; **S:** 2.5 Two-way tables

Key points

* A **two-way table** has **labelled rows** and **columns**.

* Every number is in a row and in a column so it shows **two types of information**.

* The total of all the rows is equal to the total of all the columns.

1 The two-way table shows the numbers of boys and girls in Years 9, 10 and 11.

	Year 9	Year 10	Year 11	Total
Boys	86	91	....	274
Girls	97	....	92	285
Total	183	....	....	....

Hint

Use the totals in the rows and columns to find the missing values.

Complete the table.

13

2 A hotel has different types of room available on three floors.
The two-way table gives information about these rooms.

	Standard	Superior	Executive	Total
1st floor	40	8	0	48
2nd floor	32	5	....	....
3rd floor	....	....	8	40
Total	....	17	....	130

Complete the table.

3 Carla did a survey of favourite sports.
Here are her results.

Boys

football	football	cricket	football	basketball	cricket
tennis	rugby	football	rugby	cricket	volleyball
football	volleyball	rugby	cricket		

Girls

tennis	tennis	hockey	tennis	netball
volleyball	rugby	tennis	hockey	netball
volleyball	tennis	football	netball	tennis
football	rugby			

> **Hint**
>
> Use a pencil to put tally marks in the table and then rub them out.

Complete the two-way table to show this information.

	Basketball	Cricket	Foot	Hockey	Net	Rugby	Tennis	Volley	Total
Boys									
Girls									
Total									

4 Richard asked a group of male and female students about the subjects that they were studying.
The subjects studied were English, History, IT, Languages, Maths and Sport Science. Design a
two-way table for Richard to record the number of students of each gender studying each
subject.

GCSE

5 Lizzy recorded the body-type and the colour of each car parked in a street. Here are her results.

hatch, white	estate, blue	hatch, grey	saloon, white
hatch, red	saloon, blue	saloon, white	estate, red
saloon, grey	saloon, white	estate, grey	hatch, red
hatch, blue	estate, red	saloon, red	saloon, grey

a Design a two-way-table to show this information.

b Complete your two-way table.

Needs more practice	☐	Almost there	☐	I'm proficient!	☐

Time-series graphs

GCSE LINKS
16+: Statistics 6.2 Time series

2.3

By the end of this section you will know how to:
* Draw a time-series graph

Key points

* A **time-series graph** shows how a quantity changes over time.
* Points are plotted at **equal time intervals**.
* The plotted points are joined by straight lines.
* Time is always shown on the **horizontal** axis.
* A time-series graph may include **moving averages**.
* A key is required when moving averages are included.

Guided

1 The monthly rainfall at Scarborough was recorded over a 12-month period. The results are shown in the table.

Month	Jan	Feb	Mar	Apr	May	Jun	Jul	Aug	Sep	Oct	Nov	Dec
Rainfall (mm)	55	38	48	44	51	51	52	66	55	50	60	54

Draw the time-series graph to show this information.

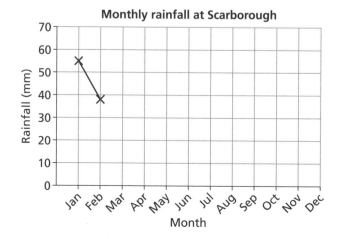

Hint

Plot the remaining points and join them with solid lines.

2 This table shows the quarterly sales of mobile phones from a shop over three years.

	Year											
	2010				**2011**				**2012**			
Quarter	1	2	3	4	1	2	3	4	1	2	3	4
Sales (000s)	13	15	21	19	14	18	24	21	16	20	25	22

a Draw a time-series graph to show the information in the table.

b Plot the 4-point moving averages on the same graph.

Moving averages:

$(13 + 15 + 21 + 19)/4 = 17$

mid-point of 1, 2, 3, 4 is 2.5,

so plot (2.5, 17)

$(15 + 21 + 19 + 14)/4 = 17.25$

mid-point of 2, 3, 4, 5 is 3.5,

so plot (3.5, 17.25)

> **You should know**
>
> Quarter 5 of the three-year period is quarter 1 of 2011. You may want to start by re-labelling the quarters in the table from 1 to 12.

> **Hint**
>
> The first moving average is the mean of the values for quarters 1 to 4 inclusive. The second is the mean of the values for quarters 2 to 5 inclusive.

> **Hint**
>
> Plot the first moving average point at the mid-point of quarters 1, 2, 3 and 4. Plot the second moving average point at the mid-point of quarters 2, 3, 4 and 5.

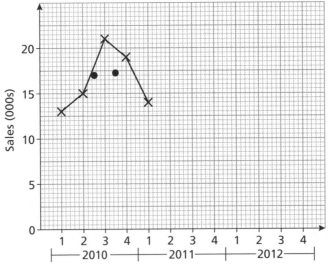

Quarterly sales of mobile phones

× Quarterly sales
● 4-point moving averages

3 The table shows the number of absences at a school over a two-week period.

Day	Week 1					Week 2				
	Mo	Tu	We	Th	Fr	Mo	Tu	We	Th	Fr
Patients	21	18	23	25	34	24	19	20	23	35

Draw a time-series graph to show this information.

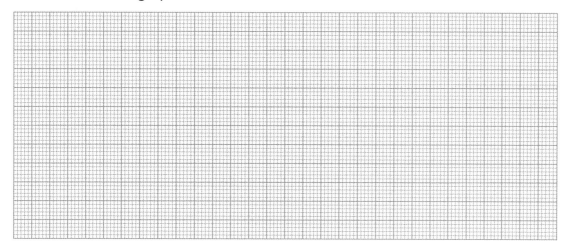

4 The table shows how sales of sun cream in the UK varied over a three-year period.

	Year											
	2010				2011				2012			
Quarter	1	2	3	4	1	2	3	4	1	2	3	4
Sales (£m)	5	22	39	11	6	24	43	9	6	17	22	8

a Draw a time-series graph to show this information.

b Plot the 4-point moving averages on the same graph.

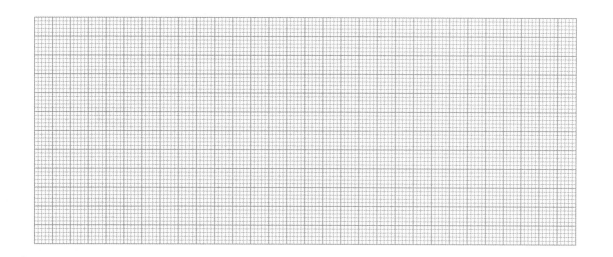

2.4 Stem and leaf diagrams

By the end of this section you will know how to:

* Write data as an ordered or unordered stem and leaf diagram
* Find the range and mode from a stem and leaf diagram

GCSE LINKS

AH: 18.3 Representing and interpreting data in a stem and leaf diagram;

BH: Unit 1 3.3 Representing and interpreting data in a stem and leaf diagram;

16+: 20.2 Constructing and interpreting stem and leaf diagrams;

S: 3.2 Pie charts and stem and leaf diagrams

Key points

* A **stem and leaf diagram** shows patterns in the data.
* Information is easier to find in an **ordered** stem and leaf diagram.
* The smallest number is given by the first leaf.
* The largest number is given by the last leaf.
* The number repeated most often in a row indicates the **mode**.

Guided

1 Here are the numbers of press-ups that some Year 11 students completed in one minute:

16   27   28   36   42   34   12   49   11   23   27   40   31   43   22   15

a Draw an unordered stem and leaf diagram to represent this information.

```
1 | 6 .................
2 | 7 8 .................        Key:  2|6 means 26 press-ups
3 | 6 .................
4 | 2 .................
```

You should know
The numbers in each row need to be put in order, smallest on the left.

b Use your answer to draw an ordered stem and leaf diagram for this information.

```
1 | 1 2 .................
2 | 2 3 .................        Key:  2|6 means 26 press-ups
3 | 1 4 .................
4 | 0 2 .................
```

Hint
Keep the numbers in tidy columns equally spaced.

2 Use your ordered stem and leaf diagram from Question 1 to find the mode of the data.

You should know
Look for the value repeated most often in a row.

Hint
When you write down the mode, use the key and remember to include the stem.

Mode = ...

3 Here is an ordered stem and leaf diagram. Find the range.

```
3 | ⑤ 6  6  8
4 | 2  3  5  7  8
5 | 1  1  1  2  5  8      Key:  5|2 means 52
6 | 6  7  9
7 | 3  4  4  ⑦
```

Hint
The first leaf and the last leaf are circled. Remember to use the key.

Hint
Take the smallest number from the largest number.

Largest number = ...   Smallest number = ...

Range = ...

4 Claire checked the pulse rates of 20 people at a gym.
Here are her results in beats per minute.

162	159	126	140	165	149	133	124	153	125
132	128	143	137	141	122	141	133	150	152

Complete the unordered stem and leaf diagram for this data.

```
12 | ..................................
13 | ..................................
14 | ..................................          Key: 14 | 3 means 143 beats per minute
15 | ..................................
16 | ..................................
```

5 Tracy asked some students how many digital albums they had.
The ordered stem and leaf diagram shows her results.

```
2 | 6   7   9
3 | 2   5   7   8   9
4 | 1   4   5   6   6   8
5 | 1   3   3   3   7   7   9       Key: 4 | 6 = 46 albums
6 | 2   3   4   4   8
7 | 2   3
```

Work out the range.

....

Find the mode.

....

6 Lily measured the heights of some students, in metres. Here are her results.

1.67	1.59	1.60	1.75	1.72	1.68	1.86	1.80	1.63	1.74	1.82	1.76	1.88	1.57	1.79
1.66	1.85	1.74	1.72	1.88	1.90	1.74	1.67	1.92	1.70	1.81	1.79	1.63	1.84	1.76

a Complete the unordered stem and leaf diagram for this information.

```
1.5 | 9   ..................................................
1.6 | 7   0   ..............................................
    |     ..................................................
    |     ..................................................          Key: 1.6 | 4 means 1.64 metres
    |     ..................................................
```

b Use your answer to draw an ordered stem and leaf diagram for this information.

7 A mechanic recorded the displayed mileage for each car serviced at a garage.
The results are shown in the stem and leaf diagram, rounded to the nearest 1000 miles.

```
1 | 4  7
2 | 1  2  2  4
3 | 2  4  5  5  5  7        Key: 3 | 7 means 37 000 miles
4 | 6  8  8  9
5 | 7  7
6 | 8
```

Find the mode.   Mode = ...

Work out the range.   Range = ...

Needs more practice ☐	Almost there ☐	I'm proficient! ☐

2.5 Grouped frequency tables

By the end of this section you will know how to:

* Complete a grouped frequency table

GCSE LINKS

AH: 11.5 Modal class and median of grouped data; **BH:** Unit 1 2.8 Modal class and median of grouped data; **16+:** 19.1 Designing and using data collection sheets; **S:** 1.9 Collecting data

Key points

* A simple **data collection sheet** has a **data column**, a **tally column** and a **frequency column**.

* **Discrete data** may be grouped into class intervals such as 1–5, 6–10 in the data column.

* **Continuous data** is always grouped into class intervals such as $0 < w \le 5$, $5 < w \le 10$ in the data column. These class intervals must not overlap.

You should know

For discrete data, 1–5 means 1, 2, 3, 4, or 5.

You should know

For continuous data, $0 < w \le 5$ includes 5 but not 0.

1 At a charity event, people were asked to guess the number of sweets in a jar.
Here are the results.

~~250~~	~~210~~	~~195~~	~~182~~	~~201~~	~~245~~	~~270~~	~~225~~	~~199~~	~~284~~
210	212	185	197	215	276	243	194	188	233
268	277	290	186	205	248	222	236	189	278
244	190	183	279	206	237	300	218	270	249

Complete the data collection sheet to show this data.

The first row of the data has been entered for you.

You should know

Tally marks are grouped in 5s as ⱶⱵⱵ

Guess	Tally	Frequency
181–200	III	
201–220	II	
221–240	I	
241–260	II	
261–280	I	
281–300	I	

Hint

There are too many different values to list them all in the table. It is better to **group** the values into class intervals instead.

Remember this

181–200 is one **class interval**. This data is grouped into six class intervals.

Guided

2 The weights of 30 bananas at a supermarket were recorded.
  Here are the results shown in grams.

146	169	141	182	178	148	163	190	172	144
163	160	172	148	184	155	169	170	183	177
147	167	142	158	167	168	179	188	172	156

Complete the data collection sheet to show this data.

Weight (w g)	Tally	Frequency
$140 < w \leqslant 150$		
$150 < w \leqslant 160$		
$160 < w \leqslant 170$		
$170 < w \leqslant 180$		
$180 < w \leqslant 190$		

You should know

The class $140 < w \leqslant 150$ includes 150 but not 140.

3 30 drivers were asked how many miles they had driven in the last week.
  Here are the results.

145	200	180	340	210	450	325	190	210	340
260	95	175	260	300	410	285	320	270	225
340	290	235	265	330	100	170	260	300	250

a Complete this data collection sheet for this information.

Number of miles	Tally	Frequency
90–100		
101–150		
151–200		
201–250		
251–300		
301–450		

You should know

The class intervals do not have to have the same width.

b Explain why it is sensible to group the data in this case.

....

....

....

4 Here are the weights, in kg, of some grey seal pups less than three weeks old.

24.3	16.8	30.7	11.2	16.0	25.4	32.6	18.5	14.9	22.7
34.4	28.7	16.5	38.6	27.9	17.2	21.3	30.4	28.7	26.4
35.3	18.6	20.4	36.2	39.5	28.3	16.8	14.8	27.1	33.6
19.2	23.6	36.6	20.0	31.7					

Design and complete a data collection sheet for this data.

Hint

Use equal class intervals, starting with $11.0 < w \leqslant 16.0$, where w represents weight.

5 Gemma records the number of emails she receives each day for 4 weeks.
Here are her results.

24	37	18	32	25	19	33
23	25	19	18	30	28	26
17	26	23	32	26	25	36
28	29	19	24	25	31	20

Number of emails	Tally	Frequency
15–20		
21–26		

Complete the grouped frequency table for the data. Use class intervals of equal width.

Needs more practice ☐   Almost there ☐   I'm proficient! ☐

Frequency polygons

2.6

By the end of this section you will know how to:

✳ Draw a frequency polygon

GCSE LINKS
AH: 18.6 Drawing and using frequency polygons; BH: Unit 1 3.6 Drawing and using frequency polygons; 16+: 21.4 Constructing and interpreting frequency polygons; S: 3.4 Frequency polygons and histograms with equal class intervals

Key points

✳ The data must be divided into **equal class intervals**.

✳ Plot the mid-point of each class interval against its frequency.

✳ Join the plotted points with straight lines.

1 Twenty Year 11 runners were timed over 100 m.
The table shows information about their times.
Draw a frequency polygon for this data.

Time (t seconds)	Frequency
$10.5 < t \leq 11.0$	2
$11.0 < t \leq 11.5$	3
$11.5 < t \leq 12.0$	8
$12.0 < t \leq 12.5$	5
$12.5 < t \leq 13.0$	2

The mid-point of the interval $10.5 < t \leq 11.0$ is 10.75

Plot the point (10.75, 2)

The mid-point of the interval $11.0 < t \leq 11.5$ is 11.25

Plot the point (11.25, 3)

You should know

The horizontal scale is continuous.

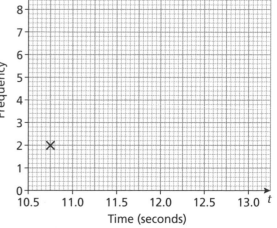

Time taken to run 100 m

2 The table shows information about the lengths l of some eels.

Length (l cm)	Frequency
$10 < l \leqslant 15$	8
$15 < l \leqslant 20$	11
$20 < l \leqslant 25$	16
$25 < l \leqslant 30$	10
$30 < l \leqslant 35$	4

Draw a frequency polygon for this data.

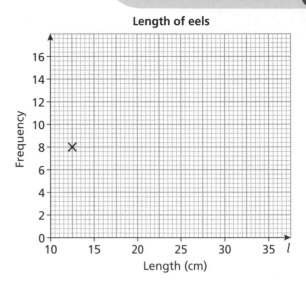

Length of eels

3 Here are the speeds v, in miles per hour, of 30 cars on the outskirts of a town.

46	33	24	35	30	25	48	41	45	43
34	28	42	48	40	39	28	47	38	44
40	36	42	48	44	47	45	48	39	40

a Summarise this data in the grouped frequency table.

Speed (v miles per hour)	Tally	Frequency
$20 < v \leqslant 25$		
$25 < v \leqslant 30$		
$30 < v \leqslant 35$		
$35 < v \leqslant 40$		
$40 < v \leqslant 45$		
$45 < v \leqslant 50$		

b On the grid, draw a frequency polygon to represent the information in your frequency table.

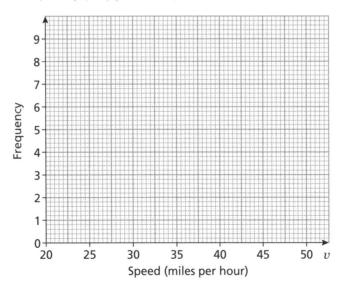

Speed (miles per hour)

2.7 Cumulative frequency diagrams

By the end of this section you will know how to:

* ✶ Draw a cumulative frequency diagram

GCSE LINKS

AH: 18.8 Drawing and using cumulative frequency graphs; **BH:** Unit 1 3.8 Draw and using cumulative frequency graph **16+:** 21.6 Constructing and interpreting cumulative frequency diagrams, **S:** 3.3 Cumulative frequency diagrams

Key points

* ✶ The **cumulative frequency** for each class interval is the **sum** of all of the frequency values up to and including that class interval.
* ✶ Plot the upper class boundary against the cumulative frequency.
* ✶ Draw a smooth curve through the plotted points.

> **You should know**
>
> The upper class boundary is the highest possible value in a class interval.

Guided

1 The table gives information about the test scores of 50 students.

Test score (t)	Frequency	Cumulative frequency
$20 < t \leqslant 30$	1	I
$30 < t \leqslant 40$	5	1 + 5 = 6
$40 < t \leqslant 50$	9	1 + 5 + 9 = 15
$50 < t \leqslant 60$	12	
$60 < t \leqslant 70$	14	
$70 < t \leqslant 80$	7	
$80 < t \leqslant 90$	2	

On the grid, draw a cumulative frequency graph for this information.

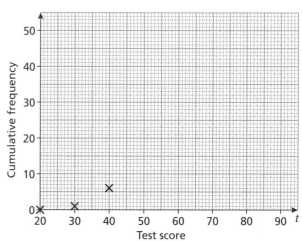

> **Hint**
>
> Remember to join the points with a smooth curve.

Practice

2 The table gives information about the birth weights of 60 babies.

Weight (w kg)	Frequency	Cumulative frequency
$1.5 < w \leqslant 2.0$	1	
$2.0 < w \leqslant 2.5$	3	
$2.5 < w \leqslant 3.0$	11	
$3.0 < w \leqslant 3.5$	24	
$3.5 < w \leqslant 4.0$	16	
$4.0 < w \leqslant 4.5$	5	

On the grid, draw a cumulative frequency graph for this information.

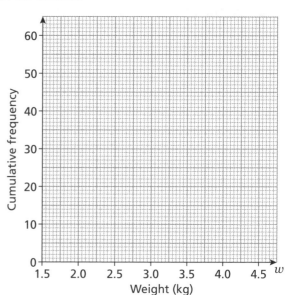

3 The table gives information about the midday temperature t at 40 locations.

Temperature ($t\,°C$)	Frequency
$0 < t \leqslant 5$	4
$5 < t \leqslant 10$	6
$10 < t \leqslant 15$	9
$15 < t \leqslant 20$	11
$20 < t \leqslant 25$	7
$25 < t \leqslant 30$	3

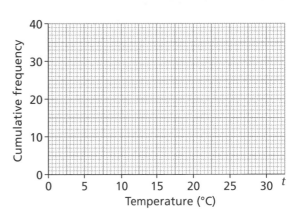

On the grid, draw a cumulative frequency graph for this information.

Needs more practice ☐   Almost there ☐   I'm proficient! ☐

Box plots

2.8

By the end of this section you will know how to:

✳ Draw a box plot

GCSE LINKS
AH: 18.10 Drawing and interpreting box plots;
BH: Unit 1 3.10 Drawing and interpreting box plots;
S: 4.9 Box plots

Key points

✳ A **box plot** has a horizontal scale.

✳ The minimum value, lower quartile, median, upper quartile and maximum value of the data are shown on the scale.

The box plot shows information about the waiting times at a doctor's surgery in minutes.

The shortest waiting time is 5 minutes.

The lower quartile is 10 minutes.

The median is 13 minutes.

The upper quartile is 17 minutes.

The longest waiting time is 25 minutes.

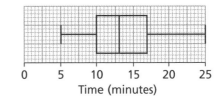

1 The pulse rates of a group of people at a shopping centre were taken.

The lowest pulse rate was 65.
The highest pulse rate was 94.
The median pulse rate was 76.
The lower quartile was 70.
The upper quartile was 85.

On the grid, draw a box plot to show this information.

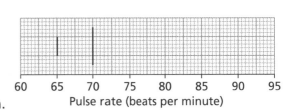

2 The table shows information about the times taken by some students to complete a puzzle.

On the grid, draw a box plot to show this information.

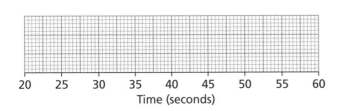

Result	Time (seconds)
Fastest	24
Slowest	58
Median	46
Lower quartile	31
Upper quartile	50

3 The table shows information about the heights reached by some rockets on Bonfire Night.

On the grid, draw a box plot to show this information.

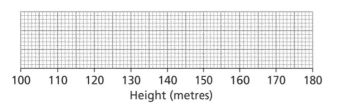

100   110   120   130   140   150   160   170   180
Height (metres)

Result	Height (metres)
Lowest	103
Highest	178
Median	136
Lower quartile	118
Upper quartile	153

Needs more practice ▢   Almost there ▢   I'm proficient! ▢

Histograms

2.9

By the end of this section you will know how to:

* Draw a histogram with equal class intervals

GCSE LINKS
AH: 18.6 Drawing and using frequency polygo
BH: Unit 1 3.6 Drawing and using frequency
polygons; 16+: 21.Constructing and interpretin
frequency polygons; S: 3.4 Frequency polygons
and histograms with equal class intervals

Key points

* A **histogram** is like a bar chart but there are no gaps between the bars.
* The bars are shown vertically.
* If the bars have the same width then the vertical axis represents frequency.
* Joining the mid-points of the tops of the bars produces a frequency polygon.

1 The table gives information about the wingspan w of 40 bats.

Wingspan (w cm)	Frequency
$15 < w \leqslant 20$	10
$20 < w \leqslant 25$	14
$25 < w \leqslant 30$	8
$30 < w \leqslant 35$	5
$35 < w \leqslant 40$	3

a On the grid, draw a histogram for this information.

b On the histogram draw a frequency polygon.

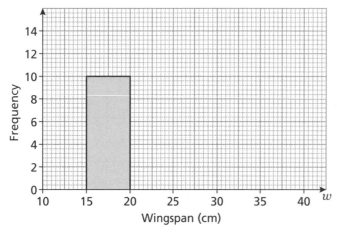

Hint

The frequency polygon is made by joining the mid-points of the tops of the bars with straight lines.

Guided

26

2 The table gives information about the times taken by 30 different objects to fall 10 m under gravity.

Time (t seconds)	Frequency
$1.4 < t \leq 1.5$	16
$1.5 < t \leq 1.6$	8
$1.6 < t \leq 1.7$	3
$1.7 < t \leq 1.8$	2
$1.8 < t \leq 1.9$	1

a On the grid, draw a histogram for this information.

b On the histogram, draw a frequency polygon.

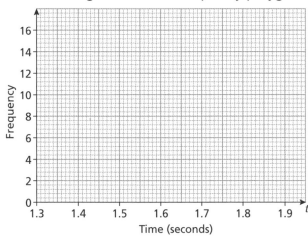

3 Here are the heights, in mm, of 30 grass seedlings.

21 27 16 12 28 20 15 19 21 15 18 20 23 11 16
12 19 25 22 27 18 12 23 17 24 18 16 13 23 22

a Summarise this information in the grouped frequency table.

Height (h mm)	Tally	Frequency
$10 < h \leq 15$		
$15 < h \leq 20$		
$20 < h \leq 25$		
$25 < h \leq 30$		

b On the grid, draw a histogram to represent the information in your grouped frequency table.

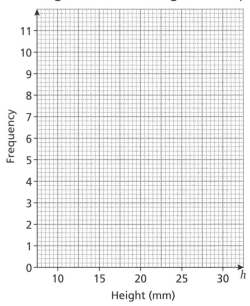

Sample space diagrams

2.10

By the end of this section you will know how to:

✳ Draw sample space diagrams

GCSE LINKS

AH: 28.1 Writing probabilities as numbers;
BH: Unit 1 5.1 Writing probabilities as number
16+: 23.3 Recording outcomes in a sample
space diagram; **S:** 7.5 Sample space

Key points

✳ A **sample space diagram** shows all of the possible outcomes of a probability experiment.

✳ The outcomes of a particular event may be identified on the diagram.

✳ The diagram may be used to calculate the probability of an event.

Guided

1 A red spinner and a blue spinner each show numbers from 1 to 4.
   The sample space diagram shows some of the possible outcomes.
   Complete the sample space diagram.

		Red spinner			
		1	**2**	**3**	**4**
	1	(1, 1)	(2, 1)	(3, 1)	
Blue	**2**	(1, 2)			
spinner	**3**				
	4				

Hint

Each outcome is shown as a pair of numbers. The first number is the value shown on the red spinner. The second number is the value shown on the blue spinner. Follow the pattern to complete the diagram.

Practice

2 A dice is rolled and a coin is spun.
   The sample space diagram shows some of the possible outcomes.
   Complete the sample space diagram.

		Dice					
		1	**2**	**3**	**4**	**5**	**6**
Coin	**H**	(1, H)	(2, H)				
	T						(6, T)

Step into GCSE

3 A dice is rolled and a four-sided spinner is spun.
   The scores are added.
   The sample space diagram shows some of the possible outcomes.

   a Complete the sample space diagram.

   b Find the number of outcomes where the total is more than 5.

		Dice					
		1	**2**	**3**	**4**	**5**	**6**
	1	2	3				
Spinner	**2**		4				
	3				7		
	4						

....

4 Three coins are spun. The sample space diagram shows some of the possible outcomes.
   Complete the sample space diagram.

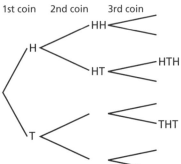

2.11 Misleading diagrams

By the end of this section you will know how to:

✳ Recognise misleading diagrams

GCSE LINKS

16+: Statistics 3.10 Misleading diagrams

Key points

Diagrams may be misleading because:

✳ they have **no scale**

✳ the scale is **not uniform**

✳ the scale **does not start from 0**

✳ the axes are **not labelled**

✳ lines may be **too thick** to take accurate readings

✳ **3D effects** may make them difficult to read.

1 The diagram below is intended to indicate that incidents of reported crime are falling.

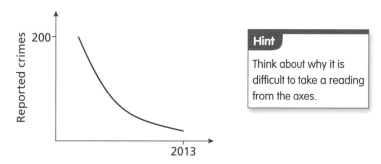

Hint

Think about why it is difficult to take a reading from the axes.

Give two reasons why the diagram is misleading.

1 ....

2 ....

2 Imagine that the Head of Sales at your company uses the graph below to show how profits have changed.

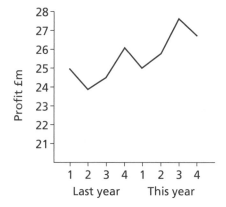

Is this graph misleading?
Give a reason for your answer.

....

....

3 Karen has been doing an experiment with a spring and some weights.
She has drawn a graph to show her results.

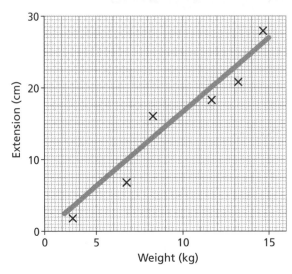

Give two reasons why you think Karen's graph is misleading.

1 ....

2 ....

4 This chart is intended to show how the number of
traffic offences in one county has changed between
2010 and 2013.

Give two reasons why the chart may be misleading.

1 ....

....

2 ....

....

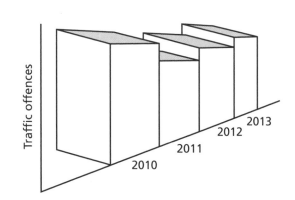

Don't forget!

∗ Composite bar charts need a .... to describe what the parts of the bars represent.

∗ In a two-way table, the .... of all the rows = the total of all the ....

∗ A .... graph shows how a quantity changes over time.

∗ A stem and leaf diagram shows .... in the data.

∗ Continuous data is always grouped into ....

∗ In a frequency polygon, the mid-point of each class interval is plotted against its

....

∗ In a cumulative frequency diagram, plot the upper .... boundary against the cumulative
frequency.

∗ The minimum value, ..., median, upper quartile and ....
of the data are shown on the scale of a box plot.

∗ In a histogram there are no .... between the bars.

∗ A sample space diagram shows all of the possible .... of a probability experiment.

Exam-style questions

1 Concrete is made by mixing cement, sand and gravel with water.
The table shows the proportions used for paths and foundations.

	Paths	Foundations
Cement	15%	10%
Sand	35%	30%
Gravel	50%	60%

On the grid, draw a composite bar chart to show this information.

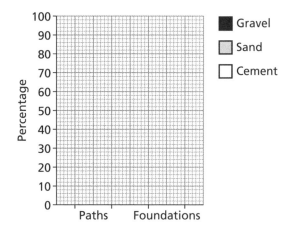

2 160 people responded to a survey about membership of a new gym. The results are shown in a two-way table.

	Junior	Adult	Senior	Total
Standard	28	26	....	75
Full	3	29	14	....
Premium	....	27	....	39
Total	32	....	....	....

Complete the two-way table.

3 The table shows the numbers of houses sold by an estate agent to first-time buyers over a 4-year period.

	Year											
	2009			**2010**			**2011**			**2012**		
Period	1	2	3	1	2	3	1	2	3	1	2	3
Houses	41	35	30	43	37	29	40	32	28	46	39	35

Draw a time-series graph to show this information.

4 Here are the numbers of rainy days in one year for 23 American cities.

134	147	126	157	158	164	158	132	159	126	148
143	123	159	158	165	154	134	137	145	135	135	158

Complete the ordered stem and leaf diagram.

12	....
13	....
14	....
15	....
16	....

Key: 14 | 7 represents 147 rainy days

5 Here are the weights w of 30 apples in grams.

195	186	210	200	198	215	220	182	190	230	235	187	204	196	197
188	182	210	205	184	181	190	192	199	206	224	235	232	196	183

a Summarise this information in the grouped frequency table.

Weight (w grams)	Tally	Frequency
$180 < w \leqslant 190$		
$190 < w \leqslant 200$		
$200 < w \leqslant 210$		
$210 < w \leqslant 220$		
$220 < w \leqslant 230$		
$230 < w \leqslant 240$		

b On the grid, draw a histogram to show the information in your grouped frequency table.

c On your histogram, draw a frequency polygon.

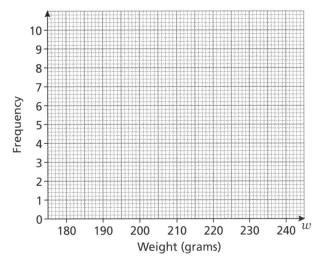

6 The table gives information about the heights h of 50 trees.

Height (h m)	Frequency
$2 < h \leqslant 3$	3
$3 < h \leqslant 4$	5
$4 < h \leqslant 5$	5
$5 < h \leqslant 6$	8
$6 < h \leqslant 7$	7
$7 < h \leqslant 8$	6
$8 < h \leqslant 9$	7
$9 < h \leqslant 10$	9

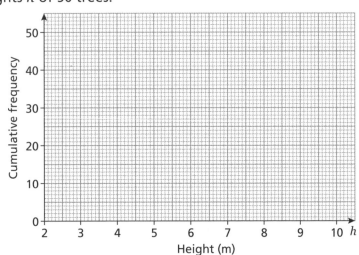

On the grid, draw a cumulative frequency graph for this information.

7 The table shows information about the times taken by some swimmers to swim 100 m.

Result	Time (seconds)
Fastest	55
Slowest	95
Median	73
Lower quartile	62
Upper quartile	77

On the grid, draw a box plot to show this information.

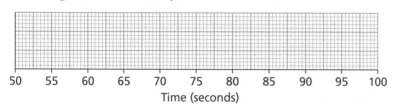

8 A red spinner and a blue spinner each have four possible outcomes: 1, 2, 3 or 4.
The spinners are spun and the difference in their scores is recorded.

a Complete the sample space diagram.

		Red spinner			
		1	**2**	**3**	**4**
Blue spinner	**1**	0	1		
	2				
	3				
	4		2		

Some of the outcomes have a difference of 2.

b How many? ....

9 This bar chart appears in a newspaper article.

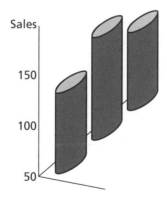

Give three reasons why this bar chart may be misleading.

1 ....

2 ....

3 ....

3.1 Calculate means for grouped and ungrouped data

By the end of this section you will know how to:

✳ Calculate the mean of data presented in different ways

GCSE LINKS

AH: 11.6 Estimating the mean of grouped data; BF: Unit 1 2.9 Estimating the mean of grouped data; 16+: 20.4 Estimating the mean of grouped data; S: 4.4 Mode median and mean of grouped data

Key points

✳ The **mean** is the sum of all the data values divided by the number of data values.

✳ To find the mean of data in a **frequency table**:
   • multiply each value by its frequency
   • divide the sum of these numbers by the sum of the frequencies.

✳ To find the mean of data in a **grouped frequency table**:
   • multiply each of the mid-interval values by its frequency
   • divide the sum of these numbers by the sum of the frequencies.

✳ The mean of data in a grouped frequency table gives an estimate of the mean as the mid-interval value is used to represent each of the values in that interval.

Finding the mean of data in a frequency table

Guided

1 Work out the mean of these eight football scores.

   3   0   2   1   5   2   1   2

   Total = 3 + 0 + 2 + ... = ...

   Mean = ... ÷ .... = ...

> **Hint**
>
> Divide the total by the number of scores.

Practice

2 Here are the numbers of letters that Tom received during one week.

   4   3   6   5   4   8   0

   Calculate the mean number of letters Tom received each day.

   Mean = ...

Step into GCSE

3 Nine runners were sponsored to run laps of the school field.
   Here are the number of laps completed by each runner.

   18   20   21   25   30   24   19   25   31

   Calculate the mean numbers of laps each person ran.

   Mean = ...

Finding the mean of data

4 The table shows the numbers of people staying in some caravans.

Number of people in caravan (p)	Number of caravans (f)	$f \times p$
1	3	3
2	5	10
3	8	
4	6	
5	2	
Total		

Hint
It is helpful to add an extra column to the table and to find the totals.

Hint
In this case, the **frequency** values are in the 'Number of caravans' column.

Find the mean number of people per caravan.

Total number of people = 3 + 10 + ... = ...

Total number of caravans = 3 + 5 + ... = ...

Mean = ... ÷ .... = ... (1 d.p.)

Hint
Round your answer to 1 decimal place.

5 Jackie went ten-pin bowling. The table shows her scores.

Score (s)	Frequency (f)	
5	1	
6	2	
7	4	
8	8	
9	9	
10	6	

Find Jackie's mean score.

Mean = ... (1 d.p.)

6 The table shows the numbers of goals scored in 20 Premier League matches.

Goals scored (g)	Number of matches (f)
0	3
1	4
2	5
3	4
4	3
5	1

Find the mean number of goals scored.

Mean = ...

Finding the mean of data in a frequency table

7 30 students in Year 11 each threw a javelin as far as they could.
The table gives information about the distances thrown in metres.

Distance (d)	Frequency (f)	Mid-point (x)	f × x
5 < d ≤ 10	5	7.5	37.5
10 < d ≤ 15	8	12.5	100
15 < d ≤ 20	9		
20 < d ≤ 25	6		
25 < d ≤ 30	2		
		Total	

Hint

The mid-point of 10 and

15 is $\frac{10 + 15}{2} = 12.5$

Find an estimate of the mean distance thrown.

Estimate of total distance = 37.5 + 100 + ... = ... metres

Estimate of mean = ... ÷ .... = ... metres

8 The table shows the midday temperature, in °C, at 25 locations in the UK on the first day of the school summer holidays.

Temperature (T °C)	Frequency (f)		
15 < T ≤ 17	1		
17 < T ≤ 19	3		
19 < T ≤ 21	8		
21 < T ≤ 23	7		
23 < T ≤ 25	6		

Find an estimate of the mean temperature.

Mean = ... °C

9 A team of 48 students ran a cross-country course of 5 miles.
The table gives information about the times taken in minutes.

Time (t minutes)	Frequency
30 < t ≤ 33	8
33 < t ≤ 36	15
36 < t ≤ 39	14
39 < t ≤ 42	7
42 < t ≤ 45	4

Work out an estimate of the mean.

Mean = ... minutes

3.2 The median and interquartile range

GCSE LINKS

AH: 11. Range, quartiles and interquartile range; **BF:** Unit 1 2.10 Range, quartiles and interquartile range; **16+:** 20.3 Constructing and interpreting cumulative frequency diagrams; **S:** 4.8 Measures of spread

By the end of this section you will know how to:

✳ Find the median, quartiles and interquartile range of ungrouped data

✳ Find the class interval containing the median of grouped data

✳ Use a cumulative frequency diagram to estimate the median, quartiles and interquartile range of grouped data

Key points

✳ For **ungrouped data** containing n values in ascending order:

- the **lower quartile, Q1,** is one quarter of the way through the data; the **position** of the lower quartile is $\frac{(n+1)}{4}$

- the **median, Q2,** is half way through the data; the position of the median is $\frac{(n+1)}{2}$

- if $\frac{(n+1)}{2}$ is not an integer, find the mean of the middle pair of numbers

- the **upper quartile, Q3,** is three quarters of the way through the data; the position of the upper quartile, Q3, is $\frac{3(n+1)}{4}$

✳ For **grouped data** containing n values:

- the median is in the class interval containing the $\frac{n}{2}$th value

- the median and quartiles may be **estimated** from a **cumulative frequency diagram**.

✳ The **interquartile range**, IQR, is a measure of the **spread** of the data; **IQR = Q3 − Q1**

✳ The IQR is more reliable than the range as it is not affected by **outliers** (extreme values).

1 Find the median, quartiles and interquartile range of this data.

| 2 | 3 | 3 | 5 | 5 | 5 | 7 | 8 | 8 | 9 | 10 |

The data is in order. There are 11 numbers.

The position of the median is $\frac{(11+1)}{2} = 6$ The median is ....

The position of the lower quartile Q1 is $\frac{(11+1)}{4} =$ ....   Q1 = ...

The position of the upper quartile Q3 is ....   Q3 = ...

The interquartile range IQR is ....

> **Hint**
> IQR = Q3 − Q1

2 Find the median, quartiles and interquartile range of this data.

| 23 | 16 | 14 | 19 | 22 | 18 | 22 |

> **Hint**
> Remember to order the data first.

Median = ...   Lower quartile = ...

Upper quartile = ...   Interquartile range = ...

3 Here are the stride lengths of 19 people in centimetres.

76	78	69	72	78	75	76	80	68	70
77	81	74	76	68	79	73	80	76	

Find the interquartile range.

.... cm

4 The cumulative frequency diagram gives information about the heights of 60 students in centimetres.

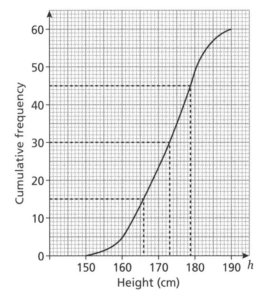

Use the cumulative frequency diagram to estimate the value of:

a the median .... cm

> **Hint**
> Start on the vertical scale at the halfway point, move across to the curve and down to find an estimate of the median.

b the lower quartile .... cm

> **Hint**
> Start on the vertical scale at one quarter of the total, move across to the curve and down to find an estimate of the lower quartile.

c the upper quartile .... cm

> **Hint**
> Start on the vertical scale at three quarters of the total, move across to the curve and down to find an estimate of the upper quartile.

d the interquartile range. .... cm

> **You should know**
> Subtract your answer for the lower quartile from your answer for the upper quartile.

5 The cumulative frequency diagram gives information about the birth weights of 48 babies.

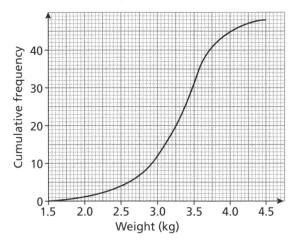

Use the cumulative frequency diagram to estimate the value of:

a the median

.... kg

b the lower quartile

.... kg

c the upper quartile

.... kg

d the interquartile range.

.... kg

6 The cumulative frequency diagram gives information about the midday temperatures at 40 locations in the UK.

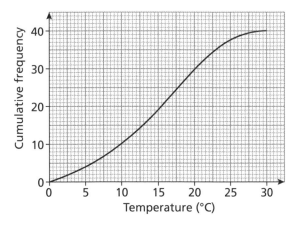

a Estimate the median.

.... °C

b Estimate the interquartile range.

.... °C

GCSE LINKS
S: 4.12 Index numbers

Moving averages and fixed-base index numbers

3.3

By the end of this section you will know how to:

* Calculate moving averages
* Combine means
* Calculate fixed-base index numbers

Key points

* A **moving average** is worked out for a given number of successive observations.
* A moving average may be used to describe a **trend**.
* The mean values of two or more collections of data may be **combined** to give the mean of all of the data.
* A **base index number** shows how the price of something changes over a period of time in relation to the price in a **base year**.

1 The table gives information about sales of barbecue sets at a shop each quarter from 2011 to 2012.

Year	2011				2012			
Quarter	1	2	3	4	1	2	3	4
Sets sold	23	86	105	16	18	45	56	15

a Calculate the 4-point moving averages for this information.

$23 + 86 + 105 + 16 = 230$ $230 \div 4 = 57.5$

Hint Find the total for the first 4 quarters. Divide this total by 4.

Hint The first moving average is 57.5

Hint Repeat the process, starting from the second quarter.

$86 + 105 + 16 + 18 = 225$ $225 \div 4 =$ ....

$105 +$ .... $=$ .... $\div 4 =$ ....

Hint Repeat the process, starting from the third quarter.

Hint Continue until the result for every quarter has been used.

The moving averages are 57.5, ..., ..., ..., ...

b Describe the trend shown by the moving averages.

....
....

Hint Decreasing averages indicate a **downward trend**. Increasing averages show an **upward trend**. Averages close in size show a **flat trend**.

Guided

2 The table gives information about the profits made by a small company from 2005 to 2012.

Year	2005	2006	2007	2008	2009	2010	2011	2012
Profit (£1000s)	142	163	170	161	167	175	168	180

a Calculate the 3-point moving averages for this information.

The moving averages are ....

b Describe what the moving averages show about the trend in profits.

....

....

3 A company designs and develops computer games. The table gives information about the number of games sold each quarter from 2011 to 2012.

Year	2011				2012			
Quarter	1	2	3	4	1	2	3	4
Games sold (1000s)	46	68	87	144	52	71	95	169

a Calculate the 4-point moving averages for this information. The first three have been done for you.

The moving averages are 86.25, 87.75, 88.5, ..., ...

b Describe what the moving averages show about the trend in sales of computer games.

....

....

4 Jack rolls a dice 10 times and has a mean score of 2.
Bella rolls a dice 15 times and has a mean score of 3.
Jack and Bella combine their results. Find the combined mean.

The total of Jack's scores is $10 \times 2 = 20$

The total of Bella's scores is $15 \times$ .... = ...

The combined total of both their scores is 20 + ... = ...

The total number of throws for both Jack and Bella is 10 + ... = ...

The combined mean $= \dfrac{\text{Combined total score}}{\text{Total number of throws}}$ $= \dfrac{.........}{.........} = $ ....

Practice

5 A class of 28 students had a mean score of 63 marks in a test.
A different class of 22 students had a mean score of 58 marks in the same test.
Find the combined mean for the two groups.

.... marks

Step into GCSE

6 A company employs 23 day-shift workers and 27 night-shift workers.
The mean weekly wage of the day-shift workers is £640.
The mean weekly wage of the night-shift workers is £720.
Find the mean weekly wage of all of these workers.

£ ....

Guided

7 The table gives information about the cost of a holiday at the same resort and at the same time of year from 2011 to 2013.

Year	2011	2012	2013
Cost (£)	876	915	998

> **Hint**
>
> Since the same base year is used, the results are called **fixed-base index numbers**.

Using 2011 as the base year, work out the index number for the cost of the holiday in 2012 and in 2013.

$$\text{Index number} = \frac{\text{Price in selected year}}{\text{Price in base year}} \times 100$$

For 2012 the index number is $\frac{915}{876} \times 100 = 104.5$ (1 d.p.)

For 2013 the index number is $\frac{........}{876} \times .... = ...$ (1 d.p.)

Practice

8 In January 2012 the average cost of a house in Staffordshire was £171 722.
In January 2013 the average cost of a house in Staffordshire was £175 329.
Using January 2012 as the base, work out the index number for the average cost of a house in Staffordshire in January 2013.
Give your answer correct to one decimal place.

.... (1 d.p.)

Step into GCSE

9 In January 2012 the cost of a litre of diesel was £1.32.
In January 2013 the cost of a litre of diesel was £1.44.
Using January 2012 as the base, work out the index number for the cost of a litre of diesel in January 2013.
Give your answer correct to one decimal place.

.... (1 d.p.)

3.4 Mean and standard deviation

GCSE LINKS
S: 4.10 Variance and standard deviation

By the end of this section you will know how to:

* use Σ notation
* calculate the standard deviation of a list of numbers
* calculate the mean

Key points

* The symbol Σ is used to mean 'the sum of'.
* Σx means 'the sum of the values of x'.
* The mean value of a set of data values is found by adding all of the data values together and dividing by the total number of values.
* The mean value of x may be written as $\bar{x}$.
* Using Σ notation, $\bar{x} = \dfrac{\Sigma x}{n}$ where n is the number of values of x.
* The **standard deviation** is a measure of **spread**.
* The standard deviation $= \sqrt{\dfrac{\Sigma x^2}{n} - \bar{x}^2}$

1 Find the mean and standard deviation of these numbers.

| 12 | 15 | 11 | 16 | 18 | 15 | 14 | 19 |

$\Sigma x = 12 + 15 + 11 + 16 + 18 + 15 + 14 + 19 = 120$　　　$n = 8$

$\bar{x} = \dfrac{\Sigma x}{n} = \dfrac{120}{8} = 15$

$\Sigma x^2 = 12^2 + 15^2 + 11^2 + 16^2 + 18^2 + 15^2 + 14^2 + 19^2 = 1852$

$\dfrac{\Sigma x^2}{n} = \dfrac{1852}{8} = 231.5$

Standard deviation $= \sqrt{\text{..........} - 15^2} = \text{.........}$ (1 d.p.)

> **Hint**
> Substitute the values into $\sqrt{\dfrac{\Sigma x^2}{n} - \bar{x}^2}$ to work out the standard deviation.

2 $n = 12$
$\Sigma x = 84$
$\Sigma x^2 = 680$

a Find the mean.

Mean $= \dfrac{\Sigma x}{n} = \dfrac{84}{\text{.....}} = \text{.....}$

b Find the standard deviation.

$\dfrac{\Sigma x^2}{n} = \dfrac{\text{.....}}{12} = \text{.........}$

Standard deviation $= \sqrt{\text{.........} - \text{.....}^2} = \text{...........................}$ (1 d.p.)

3 Find the mean and standard deviation of these numbers.

| 23 | 18 | 25 | 22 | 28 | 26 | 27 | 29 | 25 | 23 |

Mean = ...　　　Standard deviation = ... (1 d.p.)

4 $n = 16$
$\Sigma x = 176$
$\Sigma x^2 = 2400$

a Find the mean.

Mean = ...

b Find the standard deviation.
Give your answer correct to 1 decimal place.

Standard deviation = ... (1 d.p.)

5 Here are some numbers.

23   32   37   21   28   36   25   29   30

a Find the mean.

Mean = ...

b Find the standard deviation.
Give your answer correct to 1 decimal place.

Standard deviation = ... (1 d.p.)

6 $n = 18$
$\Sigma x = 450$
$\Sigma x^2 = 14\,320$

a Find the mean.

Mean = ...

b Find the standard deviation.
Give your answer correct to 1 decimal place.

Standard deviation = ... (1 d.p.)

Don't forget!

* The mean is the sum of all the data values .... by the number of data values.

* To find the mean of data in a frequency table:
  * multiply each value by its ....
  * divide the sum of these numbers by the sum of the ....

* To find the mean of data in a grouped frequency table:
  * multiply each of the .... values by its frequency
  * divide the .... of these numbers by the .... of the frequencies.

* The mean of data in a grouped frequency table gives an .... of the mean as the mid-interval value is used to represent each of the values in that interval.

* For ungrouped data containing n values in ascending order:
  * the lower quartile, Q1, is one .... of the way through the data; the position of the lower quartile is $\dfrac{(n + \text{.........})}{\text{.............}}$
  * the median, Q2, is half way through the data; the position of the median is $\dfrac{(n + \text{.........})}{\text{.............}}$

* For grouped data containing n values
  * the median is in the .... containing the $\frac{n}{2}$th value
  * the median and quartiles may be estimated from a .... diagram.

* The interquartile range, IQR, is a measure of the .... of the data.

* A moving average may be used to describe a ....

* A base index number shows how the price of something changes over a period of .... in relation to the price in a .... year.

* The standard deviation $= \sqrt{\dfrac{\Sigma x^2}{\text{.........}} - \bar{x}^2}$

Exam-style questions

1 A group of students each tried to score a bullseye on a dartboard.
The table gives information about the number of attempts they each needed.

Attempts (x)	Frequency (f)
1	3
2	4
3	8
4	10
5	5
6	4

Find the mean number of attempts needed.

Mean = ...

2 The table shows the depths of snow, in centimetres, that fell at 40 locations in the UK on the same day.

Depth (d cm)	Frequency (f)
$5 < d \leqslant 10$	2
$10 < d \leqslant 15$	3
$15 < d \leqslant 20$	6
$20 < d \leqslant 25$	9
$25 < d \leqslant 30$	12
$30 < d \leqslant 35$	5
$35 < d \leqslant 40$	3

Find an estimate of the mean.

..............................cm

3 Here are the weights of 23 apples, in grams.

176	148	169	152	138	125	146	150	168	170	144	136
177	181	174	146	125	129	155	139	146	133	162	

Find the median.

..............................grams

Find the interquartile range.

..............................grams

4 In a survey, 50 students were asked how much time they spent on the internet each day. The table gives information about these times.

Time (t minutes)	Frequency
$0 < t \leqslant 20$	12
$20 < t \leqslant 40$	15
$40 < t \leqslant 60$	16
$60 < t \leqslant 80$	4
$80 < t \leqslant 100$	1
$100 < t \leqslant 120$	2

Find the class interval which contains the median.

....

5 The cumulative frequency diagram gives information about the amounts of money that people spend on getting to work each week.

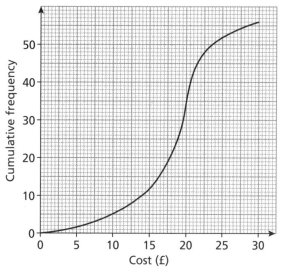

a Find an estimate for the median.

£......................................

b Find an estimate for the interquartile range.

£......................................

6 The table gives information about the number of skateboards sold by one shop each quarter from 2011 to 2012.

Year	2011				2012			
Quarter	1	2	3	4	1	2	3	4
Skateboards sold	8	15	41	12	14	19	55	10

a Calculate the 4-point moving averages for this information.
The first three have been done for you.

The moving averages are 19, 20.5, 21.5, ..., ...

b Describe what the moving averages show about the trend in sales of skateboards.

....

....

7 Ben played in 24 cricket matches in one season. He had a mean score of 16 runs per match over the first 8 games. He had a mean score of 22 runs per match over the remaining games. Find Ben's mean score for the whole season.

.... runs

8 The heating costs for some offices were £2158 in 2011.
   The heating costs for the same offices were £2347 in 2012.
   Using 2011 as the base year, work out the index number for the cost of heating the offices in 2012.
   Give your answer correct to one decimal place.

..............................(1 d.p.)

9 $n = 15$
   $\Sigma x = 615$
   $\Sigma x^2 = 31\,260$

   a Calculate the mean.

Mean = ...

   b Calculate the standard deviation.
      Give your answer correct to 3 significant figures.

Standard deviation = ...

4.1 Interpret and compare charts and diagrams

GCSE LINKS

AH: Chapter 18 Processing, representing and interpreting data; **BH:** Unit 1 Chapter 3 Processing, representing and interpreting data; **16+:** Chapter 21 Processing, representing and interpreting data; **S:** Chapter 2 Representing and processing qualitative and discrete data

By the end of this section you will know how to interpret and compare:

* Composite bar charts
* Frequency polygons
* Scatter graphs
* Cumulative frequency diagrams
* Box plots
* Histograms with equal class intervals
* Sample space diagrams

Key points

* The title or description of the diagram should contain useful information about the diagram.
* The labels give information about the quantities being described.
* Diagrams can be used to compare values or show patterns.

Composite bar charts

1 In a survey, Tom asked people from two different age groups to say which flavour ice cream they prefer from coffee, chocolate, cookie dough and vanilla. The composite bar chart gives information about their preferences.

a Which flavour was selected the most in the under-25 age group?

....

Hint

Look for the longest section in the first bar.

b Which flavour was selected the most in the 25-and-over age group?

....

c What percentage of the people in the under-25 age group selected coffee?

The section for coffee has .... vertical squares.

Each square represents ....

So the percentage that selected coffee is .... × .... = ...

d What percentage of the people in the 25-and-over age group selected chocolate?

.... %

2 The composite bar chart gives information about the numbers of red squirrels and grey squirrels in the UK between 1965 and 2010.

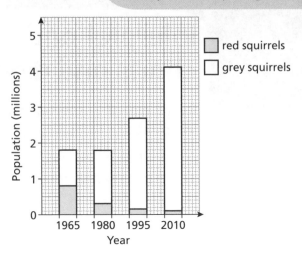

a What fraction of the squirrels in 1965 were red squirrels?

There are .... intervals representing red squirrels in 1965

There are .... intervals representing all of the squirrels in 1965

The fraction of the squirrels in 1965 that were red squirrel is $\frac{.........}{.........}$

b What fraction of the squirrels in 2010 were red squirrels?

> **Hint**
> Count each interval as 2 units. Work out the number of units representing red squirrels and the number of units representing all squirrels.

3 Jayne recorded the numbers of births of boys and girls at a maternity hospital. The composite bar chart gives information about her results.

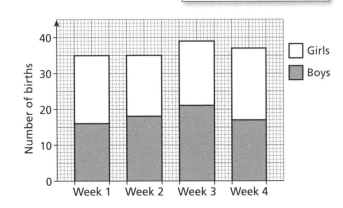

a In which week were the most births recorded?

....

b How many girls were born in Week 1?

....

c How many boys were born in Week 4? ....

d In which week was the highest proportion of boys born?

....

> **Hint**
> Write the proportions as decimals by dividing the number of boys by the number of births.

4 The composite bar chart gives information about changes in the weights of adult Americans from 1962 to 2012.

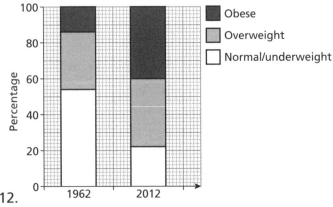

a Which was the largest category in 1962?

....

b Which was the largest category in 2012?

....

c Describe the changes between 1962 and 2012.

....

....

Frequency polygons

5 The frequency polygons give information about the times taken by a group of Year 11 students and a group of Year 7 students to run 100 m.

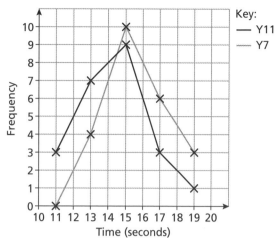

Key:
— Y11
— Y7

Make two comparisons about the times taken by the two groups.

Hint
Compare the numbers of students from the two groups who took less than 14 seconds.

Hint
Compare the numbers of students from the two groups who took more than 16 seconds.

1 ....

....

....

....

2 ....

....

....

....

6 The frequency polygons give information about the test scores for a class on each of two papers.

Make two comparisons about the scores on the two papers.

1 ....

....

....

2 ....

....

....

Key:
— Paper 1
— Paper 2

7 The frequency polygons give information about the midday temperatures at two resorts in August.

Make two comparisons about the temperatures at the two resorts.

1 ....

....

....

2 ....

....

....

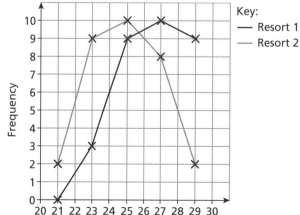

Key:
— Resort 1
— Resort 2

Scatter graphs

Guided

8 The manager of a restaurant kept a record of the number of customers served and the takings for the evening. The data for ten evenings is shown on the scatter graph.

35 customers have booked tables for tomorrow. Use the scatter graph to estimate the takings for tomorrow evening.

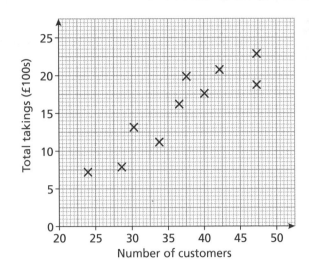

£ ....

Practice

9 The scatter graph gives information about the attainment levels achieved by some students and their marks in the end of year exam.

Lucy has an attainment level of 6.6 but she missed the end of year exam.
Use the scatter graph to estimate Lucy's exam mark.

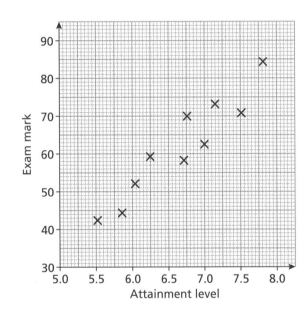

.... marks

Step into GCSE

10 The scatter graph gives information about the values of cars of a particular make in relation to their age.

Use the scatter graph to estimate the value of a 9-year-old car of this make.

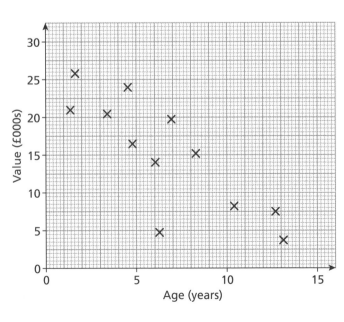

£ ....

Cumulative frequency diagrams

11 The cumulative frequency diagram gives information about the heights of 50 trees.

Use the cumulative frequency diagram to estimate:

a the number of the trees that are 5 m high or less.

> **Hint**
>
> The cumulative frequency values represent the number of trees less than or equal to a given height. Move up to the curve from 5 and read across.

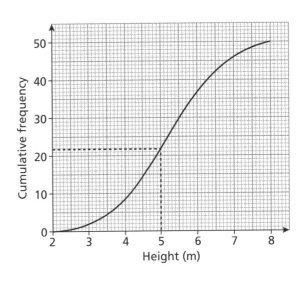

....

b the number of the trees that are taller than 6 m.

> **Hint**
>
> First, find the number of trees that are 6 m high or less. You need to subtract this from the total number of trees.

....

12 The cumulative frequency diagram gives information about the time taken to score the first goal in each of 40 Year 7 football matches.

Use the cumulative frequency diagram to estimate:

a the number of matches in which the first goal was scored in 10 minutes or less

....

b the number of matches in which the first goal was scored after 20 minutes or more.

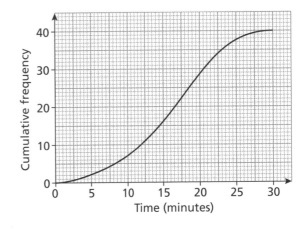

....

13 The cumulative frequency graph gives information about the marks of 50 students in an exam.

40 students passed the exam.
Use the cumulative frequency diagram to estimate:

a the number of students who achieved 65 marks or under.

....

b the pass mark for the exam.

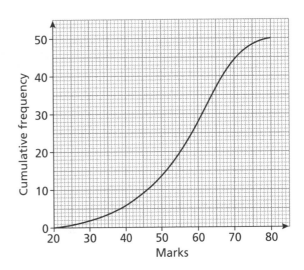

....

Box plots

Guided

14 The 'Killer Mile' is a running event held at Mow Cop in Staffordshire every year in spring. It was designed to be the toughest possible one-mile road race and includes a climb of over 550 feet. The box plot gives information about the times taken to complete the distance.

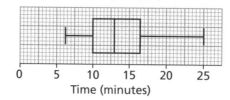

> **Hint**
> The vertical line inside the box represents the median.

a Find the median time.

.... minutes

b Work out the interquartile range.

> **Hint**
> The vertical lines at the edges of the box represent the quartiles. Subtract the lower quartile from the upper quartile.

.... minutes

15 In a survey, people were asked how much time they spent shopping online in December and in January. The box plots give information about these times.

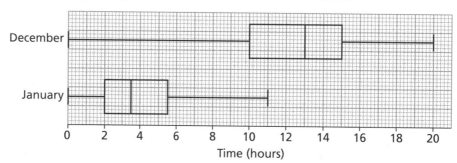

Use the box plots to compare the distributions of the online shopping times in December and in January.

> **Hint**
> Compare the medians and the interquartile ranges.

....

....

....

....

Practice

16 The lifetimes of a sample of laptop batteries were measured. The box plot gives information about the results.

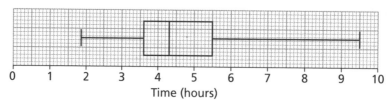

a Find the median lifetime.

.... hours

b Find the interquartile range.

.... hours

17 The box plots give information about the ages of people living in London and of people living in the rest of England.

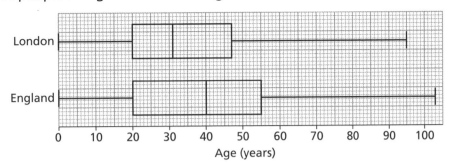

Use the box plots to compare the distributions of ages of people living in London and people living in the rest of England.

....

....

....

....

18 The box plot gives information about the distances that electric cars will travel on one charge.

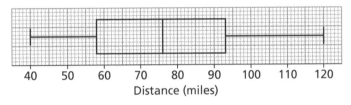

a Write down the median. .... miles

b Work out the interquartile range.

.... miles

19 The box plots give information about the monthly rainfall in London and in Milan.

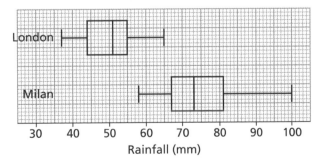

Use the box plots to compare the distributions of the rainfall in London and in Milan.

....

....

....

....

....

Histograms with equal class intervals

Guided

20 The grouped frequency table shows some information about the running times of 29 films.

Time (*t* minutes)	Frequency
$70 < t \leq 90$	5
$90 < t \leq 110$	8

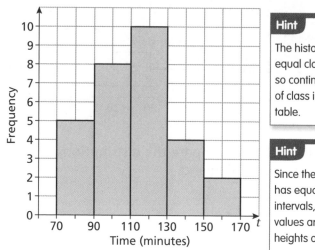

Information about these films is shown on the histogram.
Use this information to complete the table.

Hint

The histogram has equal class intervals so continue the pattern of class intervals in the table.

Hint

Since the histogram has equal class intervals, the frequency values are given by the heights of the bars.

Practice

21 Thirty students each tried to throw the highest score they could with three darts.
Information about their scores is shown in the table.

Score (*s*)	Frequency
$30 < s \leq 60$	4
$60 < s \leq 90$	

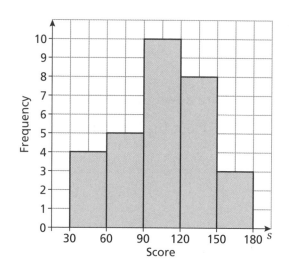

Information about the scores is shown on the histogram.
Use this information to complete the table.

Step into GCSE

22 The table gives some information about the high jump results at a school sports day.

Height (*h* m)	Frequency
$1.00 < h \leq 1.15$	3
$1.15 < h \leq 1.30$	7

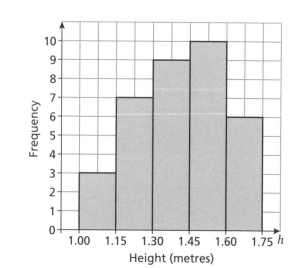

Information about the heights achieved is shown on the histogram.
Use this information to complete the table.

Sample space diagrams

23 Two four-sided spinners are spun and the scores are added. The sample space diagram shows the possible outcomes.

		Red spinner			
		1	**2**	**3**	**4**
Blue spinner	**1**	2	3	4	5
	2	3	4	5	6
	3	4	5	6	7
	4	5	6	7	8

a How many possible outcomes are there?

....

> **Hint**
>
> Each pair of scores shown in the table is a possible outcome.

b How many outcomes give a total score of 5?

....

> **Hint**
>
> Count the number of 5s shown as outcomes in the table.

c How many outcomes give a total score of 4 or less?

....

> **Hint**
>
> Count the outcomes in the table with a value of 4 or less.

24 A four-sided spinner and a five-sided spinner are spun. The difference between the scores is found. The sample space diagram shows the possible outcomes.

		Five-sided spinner				
		1	**2**	**3**	**4**	**5**
Four-sided spinner	**1**	0	1	2	3	4
	2	1	0	1	2	3
	3	2	1	0	1	2
	4	3	2	1	0	1

a How many possible outcomes are there?

....

b What is the highest possible outcome?

....

c How many outcomes have a value of 2?

....

25 A dice and a coin are thrown. The sample space diagram shows the possible outcomes.

	1	**2**	**3**	**4**	**5**	**6**
H	1,H	2,H	3,H	4,H	5,H	6,H
T	1,T	2,T	3,T	4,T	5,T	6,T

a How many possible outcomes are there?

....

b How many outcomes give an even number with Tails?

....

The modal class interval

4.2

By the end of this section you will know how to:

* Find the class interval containing the median of grouped data

GCSE LINKS

AH: 11.5 Modal class and median of grouped data; BH: Unit 1 2.8 Modal class and median of grouped data; 16+: 20.3 Using frequency tables to find averages of discrete and grouped data; S: 4.4 Mode, median and mean of grouped data

Key points

* The **modal class interval** is the class interval with the highest frequency.

Guided

1 The table shows information about the number of hours of sunshine at a resort each day in July.

Number of hours (h)	Frequency
$0 < h \leqslant 2$	3
$2 < h \leqslant 4$	5
$4 < h \leqslant 6$	7
$6 < h \leqslant 8$	9
$8 < h \leqslant 10$	7

Hint

Find the highest frequency and write down the matching class interval from the left-hand column.

Find the modal class interval.

Practice

2 Information about the lengths of some eels is shown in the table.

Length (l cm)	Frequency
$10 < l \leqslant 15$	8
$15 < l \leqslant 20$	11
$20 < l \leqslant 25$	16
$25 < l \leqslant 30$	10
$30 < l \leqslant 35$	4

Find the modal class interval.

Step into GCSE

3 Twenty Year 11 runners were timed over 100 m. The table shows information about their times.

Time (t seconds)	Frequency
$10.5 < t \leqslant 11.0$	2
$11.0 < t \leqslant 11.5$	3
$11.5 < t \leqslant 12.0$	8
$12.0 < t \leqslant 12.5$	5
$12.5 < t \leqslant 13.0$	2

Find the modal class interval.

4.3 Class intervals containing the median

GCSE LINKS

AH: 11.5 Modal class and median of grouped data; **BH:** Unit 1 2.8 Modal class and median of grouped data; **16+:** 20.3 Using frequency tables to find averages of discrete and grouped data; **S:** 4.4 Mode, median and mean of grouped data

By the end of this section you will know how to:

* Find the class interval containing the median of grouped data

Key points

* For **grouped data** containing n values, the median is in the class interval containing the $\frac{n}{2}$th value.

1 120 students took part in a Fun Run.
Information about the times taken to complete the course is given in the table.

Find the class interval which contains the median.

Time (t minutes)	Frequency
$30 < t \leq 35$	9
$35 < t \leq 40$	14
$40 < t \leq 45$	29
$45 < t \leq 50$	33
$50 < t \leq 55$	25
$55 < t \leq 60$	10

$n = 120, \frac{n}{2} = 60$

$9 + 14 + 29 = 52$

The first three class intervals contain 52 students.

The next class interval contains 33 students, so the 60th student is in this class interval.

The class interval which contains the median is ....

2 50 Emperor penguins were weighed. The table gives information about their weights.

Weight (w kg)	Frequency
$24 < w \leq 26$	3
$26 < w \leq 28$	8
$28 < w \leq 30$	11
$30 < w \leq 32$	14
$32 < w \leq 34$	10
$34 < w \leq 36$	4

Find the class interval which contains the median.

....

3 In a survey, 40 employees were asked how far they travel to work each day. The table gives information about these distances.

Distance (d miles)	Frequency
$0 < d \leq 5$	1
$5 < d \leq 10$	5
$10 < d \leq 15$	6
$15 < d \leq 20$	6
$20 < d \leq 25$	13
$25 < d \leq 30$	9

Find the class interval which contains the median.

....

GCSE LINKS
S: 4.4 Box plots

4.4 Outliers

By the end of this section you will know how to:

* Find the class interval containing the median of grouped data

Key points

* An **outlier** is an extreme value of the data.
* An outlier does not fit the general pattern of data and appears out of place.

Guided

1 Here is some data.

28   22   27   30   25   4   28   109   27

Identify any outliers.

> **Hint**
> Two of the values stand out as being different from the rest. These are the outliers.

.... and ....

2 A group of students took tests in maths and in physics. The scatter graph gives information about their results.

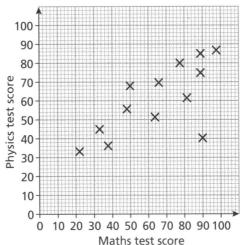

> **Hint**
> One of the points on the scatter graph stands out from the others.

Circle any outliers on the scatter graph.

Practice

3 12 students completed a science project. Here are the numbers of pages that they each submitted.

52   48   44   53   21   56   47   52   55   48   19   50

Identify any outliers.

....

Step into GCSE

4 Elaine measured the height and the girth of some trees.
The scatter graph gives information about her results.

Circle any outliers on the scatter graph.

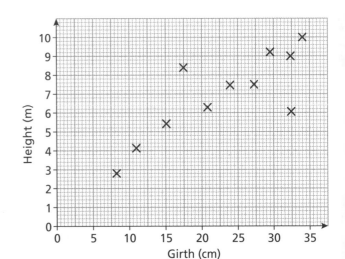

Lines of best fit and trend lines

4.5

By the end of this section you will know how to:

* Draw a line of best fit on a scatter graph
* Draw a trend line on a time-series graph

GCSE LINKS

AH: 24.4 Drawing lines of best fit;
BH: Unit 1 4.6 Drawing lines of best
fit; 16+: 22.2 Recognising correlation,
constructing and interpreting lines of
best fit by eye; using scatter graphs to
make predictions; S: 5.4 Line of best fit

Key points

* A straight line drawn to represent the plotted points on a scatter graph is called a **line of best fit**.
* There should be roughly the same number of points above and below the line of best fit.
* The direction of the line of best fit indicates the type of **correlation**.
* A **trend line** is drawn on a time-series graph in the same way as a line of best fit on a scatter graph.

1 All four scatter graphs show the same data.

Which graph shows the line of best fit?   ....

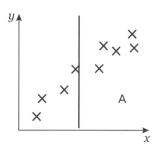

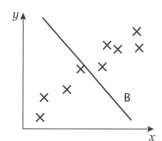

> **Hint**
>
> The correlation is positive (y increases as x increases). This rules out two of the options.

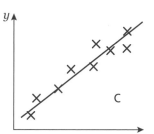

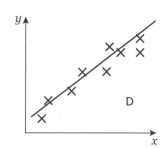

> **Hint**
>
> There should be roughly the same number of points above and below the line.

2 All four scatter graphs show the same data.

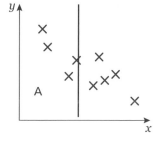

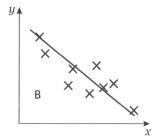

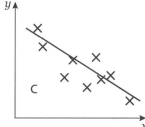

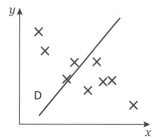

a Describe the correlation of the data ....

b Which graph shows the line of best fit? ....

3 A group of students took a test in maths and a test in physics. The scatter graph gives information about their scores. The mean maths score is 61 and the mean physics score is 59.

a Plot the mean scores.

b Draw the line of best fit.

Hint

The line of best fit must go through the mean point.

c Describe the correlation between the maths and physics scores.

....

....

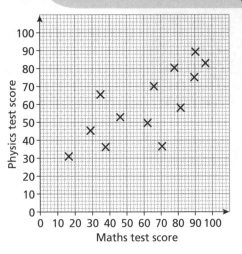

4 The time-series graph gives information about the quarterly sales of a company between 2010 and 2012.

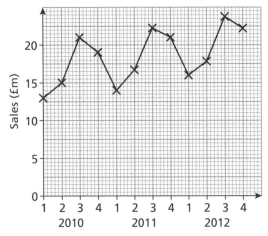

a Draw the trend line on the time-series graph.

b Describe the trend in the sales. ....

Needs more practice ☐   Almost there ☐   I'm proficient! ☐

Skew

4.6

GCSE LINK
S: 5.4 Line of best f

By the end of this section you will know how to:

✳ Identify and describe skew

Key points

✳ Data which is distributed **symmetrically** has **no skew**.

✳ Data which has more values at the higher end of the distribution has **negative skew**.

✳ Data which has more values at the lower end of the distribution has **positive skew**.

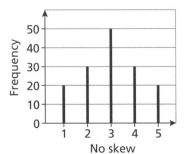

No skew

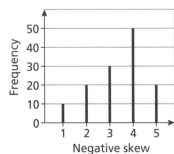

Negative skew

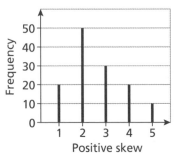

Positive skew

1 The box plot gives information about the battery life of some laptop computers.

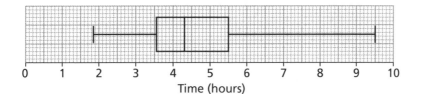

Time (hours)

Hint

The median of the data is towards the lower end of the distribution.

Describe the skew of the data. ....

2 The histogram gives some information about the high jump heights of some students at a school sports day.

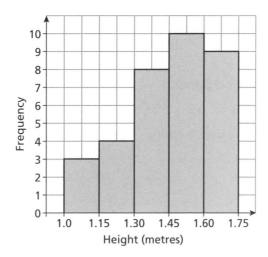

Describe the skew of the data. ....

3 The histogram gives information about the running times of some films.

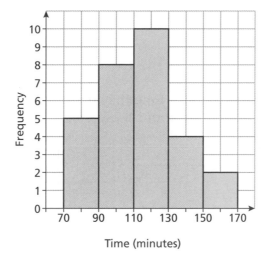

Describe the skew of the data. ....

G GCSE LINKS

S: 4.9 Bc S: 4.4 Box plots and standard deviation

4.7 Comparing data – interquartile range, skew and standard deviation

By the end of this section you will know how to:

✳ Compare data using interquartile range, skew and standard deviation

Key points

✳ **Skew** gives information about the **shape** of the distribution.

✳ The **interquartile range** measures the spread of the middle half of the data.

✳ The **standard deviation** measures the **spread** of the data using all of the data values.

Guided

1 A group of students each take two exam papers. On the first paper the mean score is 53.1 with a standard deviation of 6.4.

Here are the results for the second paper.

    48   51   67   60   48   55   72   49   56   33

Compare the scores on the two exam papers.

> **Hint**
>
> Compare the means and standard deviations of the scores on the two papers.

Σx = 48 + 51 + ... = ...

$\bar{x}$ = ... ÷ .... = ...

Σx^2 = $48^2 + 51^2$ + ... = ...

standard deviation = $\sqrt{\dfrac{\Sigma x^2}{n} - \bar{x}^2}$ =

....

....

....

2 In a survey, people were asked how much time they spent shopping online in December and in January. The box plots give information about these times.

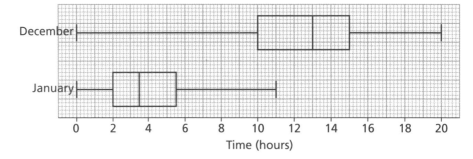

> **Hint**
>
> Use the position of the median to describe the skew for each box plot.

Compare the skew of the data for January with the skew of the data for December.

....

....

....

3 The mean weight of a litter of Golden Retriever puppies after 7 weeks is 3.6 kg with a standard deviation of 0.7 kg.
Here are the weights of some Labrador puppies after 7 weeks, in kilograms.

5.6   6.2   4.8   4.5   5.2   6.7   6.3   5.5   5.7   4.9

Compare the weights of the Golden Retriever puppies with the weights of the Labrador puppies.

....

....

4 The box plots give information about the monthly rainfall in London and in Milan.

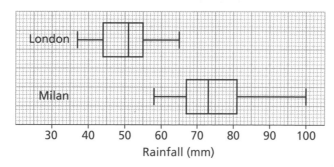

Rainfall (mm)

Use the box plots to compare:

a the skew of the data for London with the skew of the data for Milan.

....

b the interquartile range of the data for London with the interquartile range of the data for Milan.

....

5 The table gives information about the times taken by eight athletes to run 100 m at the start of the season and mid-way through the season, in seconds.

	Start of season	Mid-way through season
Σx	84.2	81.8
Σx^2	894.0	836.5

Compare the times taken at the start of the season with the times taken mid-way through the season.

....

....

4.8 Making predictions

By the end of this section you will know how to:

✳ Use a time-series graph to make predictions

Key points

✳ Repeating patterns on a time-series graph may be used to predict **short-term changes** in the future.

Guided

1 The time-series graph gives some information about the quarterly profits of a company from 2010 to the third quarter of 2012.

Predict the profit in the fourth quarter of 2012.

Hint

Follow the pattern for the fourth quarters in 2010 and 2011.

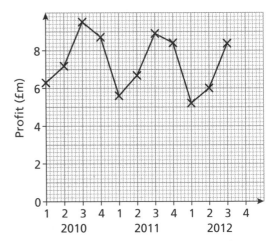

....

Practice

2 The time-series graph gives information about the quarterly sales of umbrellas from 2011 up to the second quarter of 2013.

Predict the sales in the third quarter of 2013.

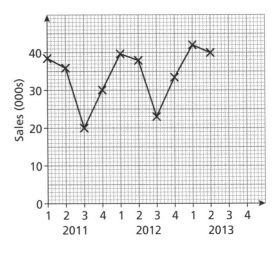

....

Step into GCSE

3 The time-series graph gives information about the quarterly sales of sunglasses at a shop from 2011 to the first quarter of 2013.

a In which quarter do you expect the highest number of sales in 2013?

....

b Predict the number of sales in this quarter.

....

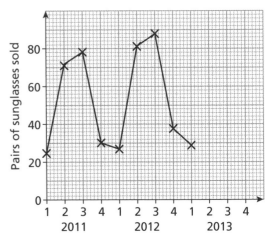

4.9 Moving averages and fixed-base index numbers

GCSE LINKS
S: 6.5 Moving averages

By the end of this section you will know how to:

* Use moving averages to describe a trend
* Interpret base index numbers

Key points

* An increase in the values of the moving averages indicates an upward trend.
* A decrease in the values of the moving averages indicates a downward trend.
* Moving averages that change very little indicate a flat trend.
* A **base index number** represents the new amount as a percentage of the amount at the time taken as the base.

1 The table shows the quarterly numbers of visitors to a builder's website during his first two years in business.

	Year 1				Year 2			
Quarter	1	2	3	4	1	2	3	4
Visitors	924	1526	1337	496	983	1496	1539	511

a Calculate the 4-point moving averages. The first three have been done for you.

The fourth moving average is $\dfrac{(496 + 983 + \rule{2cm}{0.4pt})}{4}$ = ...

The moving averages are 1070.75, 1085.5, 1078, ..., ...

b Describe the trend. ....

2 The table shows the quarterly numbers of speeding offences recorded between 2011 and 2012 along one road in Staffordshire.

	2011				2012			
Quarter	1	2	3	4	1	2	3	4
Offences	247	378	562	284	231	347	516	280

a Calculate the 4-point moving averages. The first three have been done for you.

The moving averages are 367.75, 363.75, 356, ..., ...

b Describe the trend. ....

3 The table shows the quarterly sales of pocket calculators in one shop between 2011 and 2012.

	2011				2012			
Quarter	1	2	3	4	1	2	3	4
Sales (£)	146	571	236	644	168	596	248	689

  a Calculate the 4-point moving averages. The first three have been done for you.

The moving averages are 399.25, 404.75, 411, ..., ...

  b Describe the trend. ....

4 Using January 2012 as the base, the index number for the cost of diesel in January 2013 is 109.1.

Find the percentage change in the cost of diesel from January 2012 to January 2013.

The cost of diesel in January 2013 is ....% of its cost in January 2012

This represents a ....% ....

> **Hint**
> Compare the percentage for January 2013 with 100%. Describe the change as an increase or a decrease.

5 The cost of a tablet computer in January 2013 is 8.6% less than the cost of the same tablet computer in January 2012.

Using January 2012 as the base, find the index number for the cost of the tablet computer in January 2013.

....

6 Using January 2011 as the base, the index number for the cost of unleaded fuel in January 2012 is 108.4.

  a Find the percentage change in the cost of unleaded fuel from January 2011 to January 2012.

.... %

The cost of unleaded fuel rises by 8.8% between January 2012 and January 2013.

  b Find the index number for the cost of unleaded fuel in January 2013, using January 2011 as the base.

> **Hint**
> Find the multiplier for each percentage change. Combine them to make a single multiplier for the combined percentage change. Write the corresponding index number.

....

Don't forget!

* The modal class interval is the class interval with the highest ....

* For **grouped data** containing n values, the .... is in the class interval containing the $\frac{n}{2}$th value.

* An outlier does not fit the general .... of data and appears out of place.

* A straight line drawn to represent the plotted points on a scatter graph is a ....

* There should be roughly the .... number of points above and below the line of best fit.

* The direction of the line of best fit indicates the type of ....

* A .... is drawn on a time-series graph in the same way as a line of best fit on a scatter graph.

* Data which is distributed .... has **no skew**.

* Data which has more values at the higher end of the distribution has .... **skew**.

* Data which has more values at the lower end of the distribution has .... **skew**.

* Repeating patterns on a time-series graph may be used to predict .... changes in the future.

* An increase in the values of the moving averages indicates an .... trend.

* A decrease in the values of the moving averages indicates a .... trend.

* Moving averages that change very little indicate a .... trend.

* A base index number represents the new amount as a .... of the amount at the time taken as the base.

Exam-style questions

1   There are three membership options at a gym. The composite bar chart gives information about the proportions of people taking these options in 2012 and 2013.

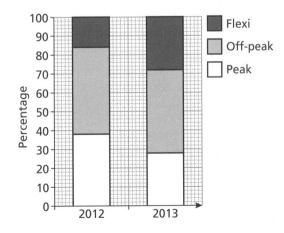

Use the composite bar chart to complete the table.

Year	Peak	Off-peak	Flexi
2012	38%		
2013			28%

2 The frequency polygons give information about the heights of some Year 7 and Year 11 students in metres.

Make two comparisons about the heights of students in the two groups.

1 ....

....

....

2 ....

....

....

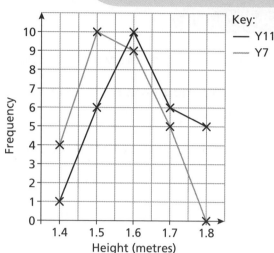

3 Information about the handspans and heights of some students is shown on the scatter graph.

  a Draw a line of best fit on the scatter graph.

  b Estimate the height of a student with a handspan of 21.5 cm.

.... cm

  c Circle any outliers on the scatter graph.

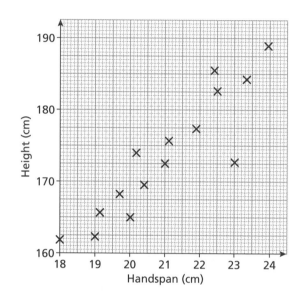

4 Contestants in a strongman competition had to hold two weights horizontally at arm's length for as long as possible.

The cumulative frequency diagram gives information about the results.

  a Estimate the median time.

.... seconds

  b Estimate the interquartile range.

.... seconds

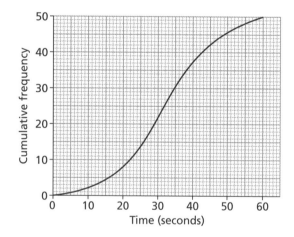

5 The box plot gives information about the times taken by a group of skiers to travel down a practice slope, in seconds.

  a Find the median time   .... seconds

  b Find the interquartile range.   .... seconds

  c Describe the skew of the data. ....

....

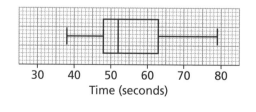

6 The stem and leaf diagrams show the test scores of two groups of pupils.

First group

```
4 | 1  3  8
5 | 2  4  5  5  9        Key: 4|1 represents
6 | 5  7  7  7  9  9           41 marks.
7 | 4  6  6
8 | 3  5
```

Second group

```
4 | 6  7
5 | 3  3  5  6          Key: 4|1 represents
6 | 4  6  8  8  8           41 marks.
7 | 3  4  6  7  7  9
8 | 1  6
```

a Compare the median for the first group with the median for the second group.

....

....

b Compare the interquartile range for the first group with the interquartile range for the second group.

....

....

7 A four-sided spinner and a dice are thrown and their scores are added.

		Dice					
		1	**2**	**3**	**4**	**5**	**6**
	1	2	3	4	5	6	7
Four-sided spinner	**2**	3	4	5	6	7	8
	3	4	5				
	4	5	6				

a Complete the sample space diagram.

b How many outcomes are there?   ....

c How many outcomes give a total of more than 5?   ....

8 A group of students each take two exam papers.
On the first paper the mean score is 48.7 with a standard deviation of 5.9.
Here are the results for the second paper.

42   59   55   63   47   58   62   49   53   40

Compare the scores on the two exam papers.

....

....

9 The table gives some information about the long jump results at a school sports day.

Distance (d m)	Frequency
$2.5 < d \leqslant 3.0$	6
$3.0 < d \leqslant 3.5$	9

Information about the distances jumped is shown on the histogram.

a Use this information to complete the table.

b Describe the modal class interval.

....

....

....

c Describe the class interval containing the median.

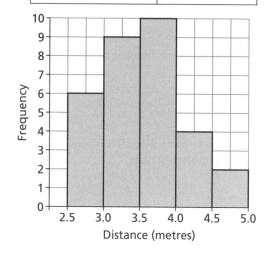

....

....

10 The table shows the quarterly sales of sun cream in one shop between 2011 and 2012.

	2011				2012			
Quarter	1	2	3	4	1	2	3	4
Sales (£)	61	168	532	125	52	146	320	95

a Calculate the 4-point moving averages. The first three have been done for you.

The moving averages are 221.50, 219.25, 213.75, ... , ...

b Describe the trend. ....

11 Using January 2011 as the base, the index number for the cost of a litre of milk in January 2012 is 106.7.

a Find the percentage change in the cost of a litre of milk from January 2011 to January 2012.

.... %

The cost of a litre of milk falls by 3% between January 2012 and January 2013.

b Find the index number for the cost of a litre of milk in January 2013, using January 2011 as the base.

....

5.1 Compare probability and relative frequency

GCSE LINKS
AH: 28.3 Estimating probability from relative frequency; BH: Unit 1 5.4 Estimating probability from relative frequency; 16+: 23.4 Using relative frequency to estimate probability and predict results; S: 7.4 Experimental probability

By the end of this section you will know how to:

* Find the probability of an event
* Find the relative frequency of an event

Key points

* If an object is taken **at random** from a collection of objects, each object has the same chance of being taken, i.e. it is **equally likely**.

* When all of the possible outcomes are equally likely, the **probability** of an event is:

Probability of an event $= \dfrac{\text{The number of outcomes in the event}}{\text{The total number of outcomes}}$

> **Remember this**
> An outcome is something that happens in an experiment, such as a dice showing a score of 6.

* If the outcomes are not equally likely, the probability may be estimated by experiment using **relative frequency**.

* In an experiment, the **relative frequency** of an event is:

Relative frequency of an event $= \dfrac{\text{The number of trials where the event occurred}}{\text{The total number of trials}}$

> **Remember this**
> A trial is something that you do in an experiment, such as rolling a dice.

* The relative frequency becomes more reliable as an estimate of the probability as the number of trials is increased.

1 Here is a five-sided spinner.

a Find the probability that the spinner will land on an even score. Give your answer as a decimal.

There are .... possible outcomes. .... of the outcomes are even.

Probability of even score = ... = ...

Ted spins the spinner 20 times. He gets an even score 7 times.

b Find the relative frequency of an even score. Give your answer as a decimal.

> **Hint**
> Divide the number of even scores by the number of spins.

Ted spins the spinner another 30 times. He gets another 14 even scores.

c Find the relative frequency of an even score using all of Ted's results. Give your answer as a decimal.

> **Hint**
> Use the total number of even scores and the total number of spins.

d Comment on your answers to **a**, **b** and **c**.

> **Hint**
> Compare the size of your answers to **b** and **c** with your answer to **a**.

73

2 A bag contains a mixture of red counters and blue counters.
Megan picks a counter at random and returns it to the bag.
She does this 40 times and picks a red counter 8 times.

    a Use Megan's results to find the relative frequency of picking a red counter.
Give your answer as a decimal.

....

    b The bag contains 100 counters of the same size and shape.
Estimate the number of red counters in the bag.

Hint

Make the probability the same
as the relative frequency.

....

3 Susan rolls an ordinary six-sided dice 24 times.
The table shows her results.

Score	1	2	3	4	5	6
Frequency	3	4	5	6	2	4

    a Find the relative frequency of scoring 5.

....

    b Find the relative frequency of scoring 4.

....

    c Susan thinks she is much more likely to score a 4 than a 5.
Is she right? Give a reason for your answer.

....

....

....

    d What could Susan do to improve the reliability of her results?

....

....

....

Practice

4 A computer is set up to display one of the numbers 0, 1, 2 and 3 at random when the spacebar is pressed. Tom presses the spacebar 12 times.
The table shows his results.

Number	0	1	2	3
Frequency	1	4	3	4

   a Tom uses the relative frequency of 0 being displayed to estimate its probability.
Write down Tom's estimate.

   ....

   b Find the probability that 0 will be displayed when the spacebar is pressed.

   ....

   c Comment on your answers to parts **a** and **b**.

   ....

   ....

   ....

Needs more practice ☐	Almost there ☐	I'm proficient! ☐

Add probabilities

5.2

By the end of this section you will know how to:

  ✱ Add probabilities

  ✱ Work out the probability that an event will not happen given the probability that the event will happen

GCSE LINKS

AH: 28.2 Mutually exclusive outcomes;
BH: Unit 1 5.3 Mutually exclusive outcomes; **16+:** 23.2 Working out the probability of an event not happening;
S: 7.4 Experimental probability

Key points

✱ You can **add** probabilities of events that cannot occur at the same time.

✱ The **sum** of the probabilities for all the possible outcomes is **1** (if the probabilities are given as decimals) or **100%** (if the probabilities are given as percentages).

✱ If the **probability** that an event will occur is **p**, then the probability it will not occur is **1 − p**.

1 A spinner has three coloured sections. The table shows the probability of landing on red or on yellow.

Colour	Red	Yellow	Blue
Probability	0.28	0.35	

Find the probability that the spinner lands on blue.

Hint

The spinner can only land on one colour. This means that the probabilities must add up to 1.

....

2 The probability that my team wins on Saturday is $\frac{5}{9}$.

Hint

You need to work out $1 - \frac{5}{9}$. It helps to write 1 as $\frac{9}{9}$.

The probability that my team does **not** win on Saturday is ....

3 The table shows the probabilities of scoring 1, 2, 3, 4 or 5 with a biased six-sided dice.

Remember this
A biased dice gives scores that are not equally likely.

Score	1	2	3	4	5	6
Probability	8%	12%	14%	25%	17%	

a Find the probability of scoring 6.

Hint
The probabilities must add up to 100%.

....

b Which score is most likely? ....

Hint
This will be the score with the highest probability.

c Find the probability of scoring 3 or 4. ....

Hint
Add the probabilities since they are mutually exclusive events.

d Find the probability of **not** scoring 1. ....

Hint
Probability of not scoring 1 = 1 − probability of scoring 1

4 The probability that it will rain in Manchester today is 0.64.
What is the probability that it will **not** rain in Manchester today? ....

5 Sara chooses a crayon at random from her pencil case.
The probability that the crayon is green is $\frac{3}{11}$ and the probability that it is blue is $\frac{4}{11}$.
Find the probability that the crayon is:

Remember this
To add or subtract fractions with the same denominator, add or subtract the numerators.

a green or blue .... b not green. ....

6 The table shows the probabilities that the Year 11 netball team will win or lose their next match.

Result	Win	Lose	Draw
Probability	42%	37%	

Find the probability that the Year 11 hockey team will:

a draw their next match ....

b **not** lose their next match. ....

7 Kath has a box of chocolates. She takes a chocolate at random.
The table shows the flavours and their probabilities of being selected.

Flavour	Toffee	Caramel	Raspberry	Truffle	Praline
Probability	0.3	0.25	0.2		0.1

a Find the probability that Kath selects a truffle. ....

b Find the probability that Kath doesn't select a toffee. ....

Kath's favourite flavours are toffee and caramel.

c Find the probability that Kath selects one of her favourites. ....

Practice

Step into GCSE

5.3 Use sample space diagrams to calculate probabilities

GCSE LINKS

AH: 28.1 Writing probabilities as numbers; BH: Unit 1 5.1 Writing probabilities as numbers; 16+: 23.3 Recording all possible outcomes of an event in a sample space diagram; S: 7.5 Sample space

By the end of this section you will know how to:

* Use a sample space diagram to calculate probabilities

Key points

* A **sample space diagram** shows all of the possible outcomes of an experiment.

* You can use a sample space diagram to identify outcomes that satisfy a condition.

1 Two four-sided spinners are spun and the scores are added.
The sample space diagram shows the possible outcomes.

		Red spinner			
		1	**2**	**3**	**4**
Blue spinner	**1**	2	3	4	5
	2	3	4	5	6
	3	4	5	6	7
	4	5	6	7	8

a Which total score is most likely? ....

> **Hint**
>
> Look for the most common outcome in the table.

b Find the probability that the total score will be 4.

The number of 4s in the table = ...

The total number of outcomes = ...

The probability that the total score will be 4

$= \dfrac{\text{Number of 4s in the table}}{\text{Total number of outcomes}} = \dfrac{............................}{............................}$

....

c Find the probability that the total score will be 5 or less.

> **Hint**
>
> This is like **b** but count the number of scores in the table that are 5 or less.

....

2 A four-sided spinner and a five-sided spinner are spun. The difference between the scores is found. The sample space diagram shows the possible outcomes.

		5-sided spinner				
		1	**2**	**3**	**4**	**5**
4-sided spinner	**1**	0	1	2	3	4
	2	1	0	1	2	3
	3	2	1	0	1	2
	4	3	2	1	0	1

a Find the probability of getting a difference of 1.

....

b Find the probability of getting a difference of at least 2.

> **Hint**
>
> 'At least 2' is the same as '2 or more'.

....

3 Sharon has two spinners.
She spins both spinners once.

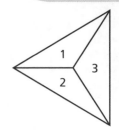
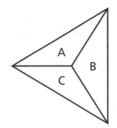

a Complete the sample space diagram.

	A	B	C
1	(A, 1)	(B, 1)	(C, 1)
2	(A, 2)	(B, 2)	
3			

b Find the probability that Sharon gets the letter A with an odd number.

....

Needs more practice ☐	Almost there ☐	I'm proficient! ☐

5.4 Use probability to estimate outcomes

GCSE LINKS

AH: 28.4 Finding the expected number of outcomes; **BH:** Unit 1 5.5 Finding the expected number of outcomes; **16+:** 23.4 Using relative frequency to estimate probability and predict results; **S:** 7.4 Experimental probability

By the end of this section you will know how to:

＊ Use relative frequency to estimate probability

＊ Predict the number of times an event will occur

Key points

＊ Repeating an experiment will usually produce different outcomes.

＊ The **predicted** number of times an event will occur
= the **probability** of the event × the **number of trials**.

1 Josh rolls an ordinary dice 30 times. Estimate the number of times that he will get a score of 4.

Probability of a score of 4 = $\frac{\text{.........}}{6}$

Expected number of 4s = $\frac{\text{.........}}{6}$ × .... = ...

2 Kate plants 80 seeds and finds that 63 of them germinate.

a A seed of the same type is selected at random.
Estimate the probability that it will germinate.
Give your answer as a decimal.

> **Hint**
> Use relative frequency.
> 63 out of 80 seeds germinate.
> Work out 63 ÷ 80.

....

b Kate plants another 200 seeds.
Estimate the number of these seeds that will germinate.

> **Hint**
> Use your estimate of the probability from **a**.
> Multiply it by the number of trials. In this case,
> each seed planted is a trial.

....

3 At a set of traffic lights, cars can only turn left or right.
In a survey of 50 cars, 30 turned left.

   a Estimate the probability that the next car will turn left.
   Give your answer as a decimal.

   ....

   b Of the next 70 cars, how many would you estimate will turn left?

   ....

4 Two coins are spun. The sample space diagram shows the possible outcomes.

		First coin	
		H	**T**
Second coin	**H**	H, H	T, H
	T	H, T	T, T

   a Find the probability that both coins will land on Heads.   ....

   The coins are spun 60 times.

   b Estimate the number of times that both coins will land on Heads.   ....

5 The table shows the probabilities that a four-sided spinner will land on blue, red or yellow.

Colour	Blue	Green	Red	Yellow
Probability	16%		35%	29%

   a Work out the probability that the spinner will land on green.

   ....%

   Lucy is going to spin the spinner 50 times.

   b Work out an estimate of the number of times that the spinner will land on blue.

   ....

5.5 Multiply probabilities using tree diagrams

GCSE LINKS

AH: 28.6 Probability tree diagram
BH: Unit 1 5.7 Probability tree diagrams; 16+: 23.5 Completing and using a probability tree diagram; S: 7.12 Tree diagrams

By the end of this section you will know how to:

* Complete a probability tree diagram
* Use a probability tree diagram to calculate probabilities

Key points

* A **probability tree diagram** shows the probabilities of successive events.
* Probabilities on branches that meet at a point add up to 1 or 100%.
* To find the probability of a sequence of events, multiply the probabilities on the corresponding branches.

Guided

1 Sophie picks a card at random from a pack of playing cards. She returns the card to the pack and picks a second card at random. Each time, Sophie is hoping to pick a Club.

a Complete the tree diagram.

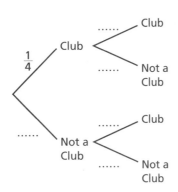

First card   Second card

Hint

Sophie always replaces the card in the pack, so the probabilities for the second card are the same as for the first card.

Hint

Each card is either a Club or not a Club.

Each time:

Probability of 'Not a Club' = 1 − .... = ...

b Find the probability that neither card is a club.

Hint

There are two probabilities to multiply.

....

Practice

2 Three coins are spun.

a Complete the probability tree diagram.

b Work out the probability that all three coins land on Heads.

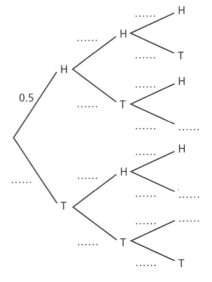

1st coin   2nd coin   3rd coin

3 Amy is going to take two exams.
The probability that she will pass the first exam is 0.84
The probability that she will pass the second exam is 0.75

   a Complete the probability tree diagram.

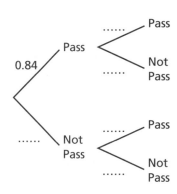

First exam   Second exam

   b Find the probability that Amy will pass both exams.

....

Don't forget!

✱ If an object is taken at random from a collection of objects, each object has the .... chance of being taken.

✱ When all of the possible outcomes are equally likely, the probability of an event is:

   Probability of an event = $\dfrac{\text{The number of outcomes in ....}}{\text{The .... number of outcomes}}$

✱ If the outcomes are not equally likely, the probability may be .... by experiment using relative frequency.

✱ In an experiment, the relative frequency of an event is:

   Relative frequency of an event = $\dfrac{\text{The number of trials where the ....}}{\text{The total number of ....}}$

✱ The relative frequency becomes more reliable as an estimate of the probability as the number of trials is ....

✱ You can add probabilities of events that cannot occur at ....

✱ The sum of the probabilities for all the possible outcomes is .... or ....

✱ If the probability that an event will occur is p, then the probability it will not occur is ....

✱ A sample space diagram shows all of the possible .... of an experiment.

✱ Repeating an experiment will usually produce .... outcomes.

✱ The predicted number of times an event will occur
   = the probability of the event × ....

✱ A probability tree diagram shows the probabilities of .... events.

✱ Probabilities on branches that meet at a point add up to ....

✱ To find the probability of a sequence of events, ... the probabilities on the corresponding branches.

Exam-style questions

1 Erica has 7 red cards and 3 black cards. She picks at random a card, then she records the colour and puts it back in the pack. She does this 50 times.
The table shows her results.

Red	Black
33	17

   a Work out the relative frequency of Erica picking a red card.
     Give your answer as a decimal.

     ....

   b Find the probability that a card picked at random will be red.
     Give your answer as a decimal.

     ....

2 Nick is playing golf. The table shows some probabilities based on his first shot from the tee.
For each shot, there are four possible outcomes for where the ball lands.

Green	Fairway	Rough	Bunker
4%	79%	12%	

   a What is the probability of Nick's shot landing in a bunker?

     ....

   b What is the probability that the ball lands on the green or on the fairway?

     ....

In one week, Nick plays from the tee 90 times.

   c Work out an estimate for the number of times that the ball lands in the rough.

     ....

3 Here are two spinners.
Each time that they are spun, the scores are added.

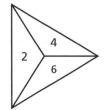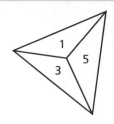

	2	4	6
1	3		
3			
5		9	

a Complete the sample space diagram.

b Work out the probability that the total score is 5.

....

c Work out the probability that the total score is more than 3.

....

Toby spins the spinners 45 times.

d Work out an estimate for the number of times Toby has a total score of more than 3.

....

4 Sharon throws an ordinary dice twice. She hopes to avoid a score of 6

a Complete the tree diagram.

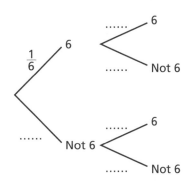

First throw   Second throw

$\frac{1}{6}$ 6

...... 6

...... Not 6

...... Not 6

...... 6

...... Not 6

b Work out the probability that Sharon will not get a 6 on both throws.

....

Practice Paper

Time: 1 hour 30 minutes

Edexcel publishes Sample Assessment Material on its website. This Practice Exam Paper has been written to help you practise what you have learned and may not be representative of a real exam paper.

1   There are different types of data:

discrete	continuous	categorical

Complete the table.

Variable	Type of data
Speed of a car	
Shoe size	
The number of teachers in a school	
The make of a computer	

(Total for Question 1 is 4 marks)

---

2   Here are the numbers of calories in a sample of 30 ready-meals.

1024	976	1210	1105	1153	926	1253	1167	1327	1245
918	1025	1247	1133	1248	996	1000	1324	1178	1289
1176	1356	1122	1019	945	936	1247	1035	1258	1036

a Summarise the data in the grouped frequency table.   (2)

Calories (x)	Tally	Frequency
$900 < x \leqslant 1000$		
$1000 < x \leqslant 1100$		
$1100 < x \leqslant 1200$		
$1200 < x \leqslant 1300$		
$1300 < x \leqslant 1400$		

b Write down the modal class interval.

....
(1)

c Find the class interval which contains the median.

....
(1)

(Total for Question 2 is 4 marks)

3 Gareth wants to know how people feel about the proposal to build some new houses on part of a town centre car park.

   a Design a question that Gareth could use in his questionnaire.
You must include some response boxes.

(2)

Gareth plans to give the questionnaire to shopkeepers with premises next to the car park.

b Write down one reason why this may **not** be a good sample.

....

....

(1)

(Total for Question 3 is 3 marks)

4 Jake has a biased coin.
The probability that the coin will land on Heads is 0.64
Jake spins the coin twice.

   a Complete the tree diagram.

First spin   Second spin

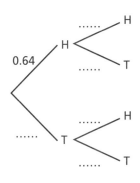

(2)

b Find the probability that the coin will land on Heads on the first spin and on the second spin.

....

(2)

(Total for Question 4 is 4 marks)

5 In a survey, ramblers at a Visitor Centre in the Lake District were asked how far they had walked that day.
The table gives information about the responses.

Distance walked (x miles)	Frequency
$0 < x \leqslant 2$	2
$2 < x \leqslant 4$	3
$4 < x \leqslant 6$	9
$6 < x \leqslant 8$	10
$8 < x \leqslant 10$	8

a Draw a histogram to show this information.

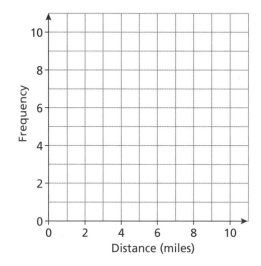

(2)

b Describe the skew.

....

(1)

c Work out an estimate of the mean distance walked.

.... miles

(2)

d One person is picked at random.
Find the probability that this person walked more than 6 miles.

....

(2)

(Total for Question 5 is 7 marks)

6 At a Christmas Fayre, people were asked to estimate the weight, in kilograms, of a Christmas cake. Here are the results.

2.3	1.5	4.2	3.5	4.2	2.7	3.9	5.0	2.7
4.3	5.2	3.7	3.9	5.2	4.6	3.3	4.8	2.6
5.8	3.4	2.6	3.7	4.8	4.2	3.7	5.4	4.0

a Draw an ordered stem and leaf diagram to show this information.

(3)

b Find the median.

....

(1)

c Find the interquartile range.

....

(1)

d On the grid, draw a box plot for the information.

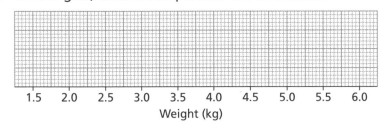

Weight (kg)

(2)

(Total for Question 6 is 7 marks)

7 Emily has a five-sided spinner. The spinner is biased.
The table shows the probabilities that the spinner will land on 1, on 2, on 4 or on 5.

Number	1	2	3	4	5
Probability	0.18	0.16		0.15	0.21

a Work out the probability that the spinner will land on 3.

....

(2)

Emily spins the spinner 40 times.

b Work out an estimate of the number of times the spinner lands on 3.

....

(1)

(Total for Question 7 is 3 marks)

8 The cost of a barrel of oil in January 2011 was £55.28.
The cost of a barrel of oil in January 2012 was £59.84.

    a Using January 2011 as the base year, work out the index number for the cost of a barrel of oil in January 2012.

....

(2)

    b Interpret your index number in **a**.

....

(2)

(Total for Question 8 is 4 marks)

---

9 Two maths sets took the same exam paper. The table gives some information about their results.

Work out the mean mark of the 58 students.

	Number of students	Mean mark
Set 1	30	64
Set 2	28	55

....

(Total for Question 9 is 3 marks)

---

10 A spinner can land on Red (R), on White (W) or on Blue (B). It has an equal chance of landing on each colour.
James spins the spinner twice.
The sample space diagram shows some of the possible outcomes.

		First spin		
		R	W	B
Second spin	R	(R, R)	(W, R)	(B, R)
	W	(R, W)		
	B	(R, B)		

    a Complete the sample space diagram. (2)

    b Find the probability that the spinner lands on Red on the first spin and on the second spin.

....

(1)

    c Find the probability that the spinner lands on a different colour each time.

....

(1)

(Total for Question 10 is 4 marks)

11 Here are the times taken, in minutes, for 15 vehicles to travel North between two junctions on the M6 motorway.

    18   15   21   18   23   22   19   20
    23   17   20   21   20   18   17

For vehicles travelling South between the same two junctions:
    The median is 22 minutes.
    The interquartile range is 5 minutes.
Compare the times taken to travel North with the times taken to travel South between the two motorway junctions.

(Total for Question 11 is 4 marks)

12 The table shows the numbers of students in Year 9, in Year 10 and in Year 11 at a school.

	Year 9	Year 10	Year 11
Number of students	115	119	126

A sample of 40 students is taken.
The sample is stratified by year group.
Work out the number of Year 11 students in the sample.

(Total for Question 12 is 2 marks)

13 Sam wants to know if the people of a town are in favour of having an extra supermarket.
He asks a sample of people from the town.
Write down one advantage of taking a sample.

(Total for Question 13 is 1 mark)

14 The scatter graph gives information about the temperature and height at different points on Ben Nevis on one day in April.

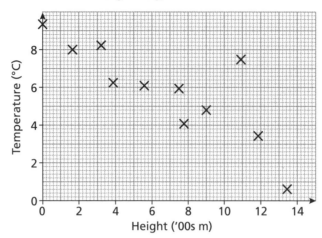

a On the grid, circle the possible outlier. (1)

b On the grid, draw a line of best fit for this information. (1)

c Estimate the temperature at a height of 1000 m.

....°C

(1)

d Describe the relationship between height and temperature.

....

....

(1)

(Total for Question 14 is 4 marks)

---

15 The table gives information about the number of pairs of Wellingtons sold by a shop in each quarter from 2011 to 2012.

Year	2011				2012			
Quarter	1	2	3	4	1	2	3	4
Number of pairs of Wellingtons	310	189	212	325	316	235	232	329

a Calculate the 4-point moving averages for this information.
The first three have been done for you.

259, 260.5, 272, ...

(2)

b Describe the trend.

....

....

(1)

(Total for Question 15 is 3 marks)

16 Sally rolls a fair four-sided dice 10 times.
The table shows her results.

Score	1	2	3	4
Frequency	3	1	4	2

a Find the relative frequency of scoring 4.

....

(1)

b Find the probability of scoring 4.

....

(1)

c Comment on your answers to **a** and **b**.

....

....

(1)

(Total for Question 16 is 3 marks)

17 The diagram shows the profit made by a company each year
from 2010 to 2012.

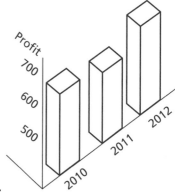

Write down three things about the diagram that could be misleading.

1 ....

2 ....

3 ....

(Total for Question 17 is 3 marks)

18 30 words were selected at random from Book A. 30 words were
then selected at random from Book B. The frequency polygons
give information about the numbers of letters used in the
selected words.

Make two comparisons about the selected words from Book A
and from Book B.

1 ....

....

....

2 ....

....

....

(Total for Question 18 is 2 marks)

19 Geoff picks a shirt at random from his wardrobe.

The probability that he picks a white shirt is $\frac{3}{5}$.

The probability that he picks a blue shirt is $\frac{3}{10}$.

a Find the probability that Geoff picks a white shirt or a blue shirt.

....

(2)

b Find the probability that Geoff picks a shirt that is not blue.

....

(2)

(Total for Question 19 is 4 marks)

20 The table gives information about the times taken by 50 students to complete a cross-country course.

Time (x minutes)	Frequency
$20 < x \leqslant 22$	7
$22 < x \leqslant 24$	12
$24 < x \leqslant 26$	16
$26 < x \leqslant 28$	9
$28 < x \leqslant 30$	6

a On the grid, draw a cumulative frequency graph for this information.

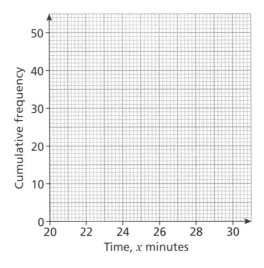

(3)

b Use your cumulative frequency graph to find an estimate of the number of students who took more than 25 minutes.

....

(2)

(Total for Question 20 is 5 marks)

21 The time-series graph shows the number of swimming costumes sold in a shop each quarter from 2011 to the second quarter of 2013.

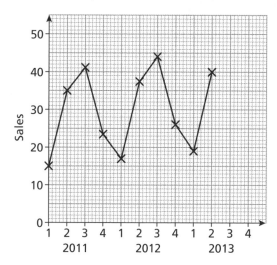

Predict the number of sales in the third quarter of 2013.

....

(Total for Question 21 is 2 marks)

22 $n = 25$
$\Sigma x = 78$
$\Sigma x^2 = 292$

a Calculate the mean.

....

(2)

b Calculate the standard deviation.
Give your answer correct to 3 decimal places.

....

(2)

(Total for Question 22 is 4 marks)

TOTAL FOR PAPER IS 80 MARKS

Answers

1 Data

1.1 Types of data

1. Categorical – D
   Discrete – C, E, F
   Continuous – A, B, G
2. **a** Categorical
   b Continuous
   c Categorical
3. **a** Discrete
   b Categorical
4. Type of fish – categorical
   Length – continuous
   Weight – continuous
5. Type of bird – categorical
   Number seen – discrete

6.

	Data type		
Data	Categorical	Discrete	Continuous
The temperature inside a fridge			✓
The makes of car in a car park	✓		
The number of people at a cricket match		✓	
The colours of sweets in a jar	✓		
The area of a rectangle			✓

1.2 Sampling

1. **a** The complete batch of loaves
   b Taking a census would mean that none of the loaves in a batch could be sold. Taking a sample provides information without destroying the batch.
2. **a** All of the drivers that pass through the toll gate
   b There would only be enough time to take a sample.
3. **a** People in the UK who watch television
   b The population is too large to take a census.
4. **a** All of the exam papers marked by the examiner
   b There is not enough time for the lead examiner to re-mark all of the papers.

1.3 Design a question for a questionnaire

1. **a** The words 'Do you agree ...' suggest which answer is expected.
   b Your answer should mention that some people may be embarrassed by the question.
   c Your answer should refer to the fact that there is no clear difference between some of the responses.
   d You should mention that some of the responses overlap.
2. **a** Do you agree or disagree that students should be able to use the computer room at lunchtime?
   ☐ Agree
   ☐ Disagree
   ☐ Don't know
   b Which of these meals is your favourite?
   ☐ Salad
   ☐ Fish and chips
   ☐ A pasta dish
   ☐ Curry
   ☐ None of these

c How much time do you usually spend on homework in a week?
   ☐ 0−3 hours
   ☐ 4−6 hours
   ☐ 7−9 hours (or 7−10 hours)
   ☐ More than 9 hours (or More than 10 hours)
d Do you think that revision guides are helpful?
   ☐ Yes
   ☐ No
   ☐ Don't know

3. **a** The responses '5 or 6' and '6 or 7' overlap.
   How many times a week do you eat bread?
   ☐ Less than 5
   ☐ 5 or 6
   ☐ 7 or 8
   ☐ More than 8
   b The question is too difficult for many people to answer. Think about reducing the number of options or changing the categories to something non-numerical.
   c This is a leading question. You need to remove the bias. This could be done by replacing 'agree' with 'think' or 'agree or disagree'.
4. **a** There is no option for people who don't like the product.
   b How do you rate this product?
   ☐ Excellent
   ☐ Very good
   ☐ Good
   ☐ Not very good
   ☐ Poor
5. Please indicate how happy you are with the quality of service.
   ☐ Completely satisfied
   ☐ Satisfied
   ☐ Unsatisfied
   ☐ Completely unsatisfied

1.4 Bias in sampling methods

1. The survey is taken on a market day so many people in the town will be there for the market. Their views may not represent the views of the town population.
2. The views of people walking their dogs are likely to indicate that dogs should not have to be muzzled.
3. The only teachers still there at the end of the day will be the ones who have found the talks useful.
4. It is unlikely that many teenagers will have a chance to take part in the survey.
5. The people leaving the cinema are likely to have similar views about the movies that they like to see. These views may not be the same as those of the general public.
6. **a** 1 The sample size is too small.
   2 The timing of the survey may affect who is available to give their views.
   b 1 Increase the sample size.
   2 Ask people at a variety of locations and at different times.

1.5 Calculate a stratified sample

1. Group size = 35
   Population size = 25 + 35 = 60
   Number of girls in sample = $\frac{35}{60} \times 12 = 7$
2. 14 full-time members
3. 3 large coats
4. 10 people

Don't forget!

* specific
* numerical; range
* words; numbers
* represent
* purpose
* biased
* population
* equal
* strata
* proportion

Exam-style questions

1

Data collected	Data type
Make and model	Categorical
Number of passenger seats	Discrete

2 Do you agree or disagree that Year 11 students should always be allowed an early lunch?

☐ Agree ☐ Disagree ☐ Don't know

3 1 People in his class are unlikely to represent the population.
    2 The sample size is too small.

4 5 KS5 students

2 Displaying data

2.1 Composite bar charts

1

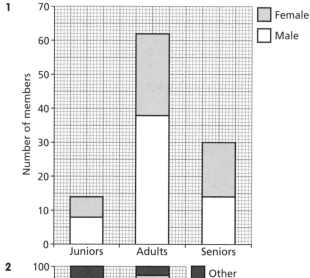

2

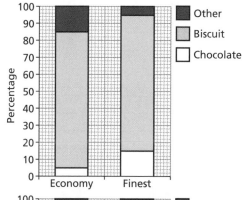

3

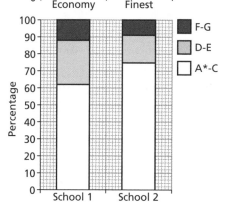

2.2 Two-way tables

1

	Year 9	Year 10	Year 11	Total
Boys	86	91	97	274
Girls	97	96	92	285
Total	183	187	189	559

2

	Standard	Superior	Executive	Total
1st floor	40	8	0	48
2nd floor	32	5	5	42
3rd floor	28	4	8	40
Total	100	17	13	130

3

	Basket	Cricket	Foot	Hockey	Net	Rugby	Tennis	Volley	Total
Boys	1	4	5	0	0	3	1	2	16
Girls	0	0	2	2	3	2	6	2	17
Total	1	4	7	2	3	5	7	4	33

4

	English	History	IT	Languages	Maths	Sport Science	Total
Male							
Female							
Total							

5

	Hatch	Estate	Saloon	Total
Blue	1	1	1	
Grey	1	1	2	
Red	2	2	1	
White	1	0	3	
Total				

2.3 Time-series graphs

1

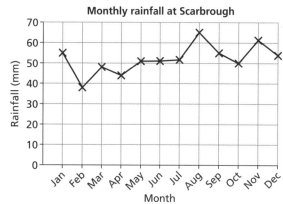

2

3

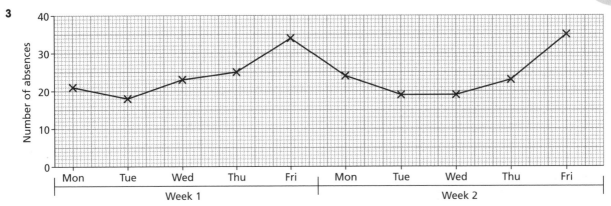

4

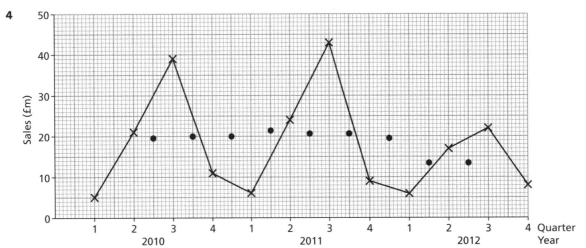

2.4 Stem and leaf diagrams

1 a

1	6	2	1	5
2	7	8	3	7	2
3	6	4	1
4	2	9	0	3

Key: 2 | 6 means
26 press-ups

b

1	1	2	5	6
2	2	3	7	7	8
3	1	4	6
4	0	2	3	9

Key: 2 | 6 means
26 press-ups

2 Mode = 27

3 Largest number = 77, Smallest number = 35, Range = 42

4

12	6	4	5	8	2
13	3	2	7	3
14	0	9	3	1	1
15	9	3	0	2
16	2	5

Key: 14 | 3 means 143 beats
per minute

5 Range = 47, Mode = 53

6 a

1.5	9	7
1.6	7	0	8	3	6	7	3
1.7	5	2	4	6	9	4	2	4	0	9	6
1.8	6	0	2	8	5	8	1	4
1.9	0	2

Key:
1.6 | 4
means
1.64
metres

b

1.5	7	9
1.6	0	3	3	6	7	7	8
1.7	0	2	2	4	4	4	5	6	6	9	9
1.8	0	1	2	4	5	6	8	8
1.9	0	2

Key:
1.6 | 4
means
1.64
metres

7 Mode = 35 000 miles, Range = 54 000 miles

2.5 Grouped frequency tables

1

Guess	Tally	Frequency
181–200	ЖЖI	11
201–220	ЖIII	8
221–240	Ж	5
241–260	ЖI	6
261–280	ЖII	7
281–300	III	3

2

Weight (w g)	Tally	Frequency
140 < w ≤ 150	ЖII	7
150 < w ≤ 160	IIII	4
160 < w ≤ 170	ЖIII	8
170 < w ≤ 180	ЖI	6
180 < w ≤ 190	Ж	5

3 a

Number of miles	Tally	Frequency
90–100	II	2
101–150	I	1
151–200	Ж	5
201–250	Ж	5
251–300	ЖIIII	9
301–450	ЖIII	8

b There are too many different values to show them in an
ungrouped frequency table.

4

Weight (w kg)	Tally	Frequency
11.0 < w ≤ 16.0	IIII	4
16.0 < w ≤ 21.0	ЖIIII	9
21.0 < w ≤ 26.0	Ж	5
26.0 < w ≤ 31.0	ЖIII	8
31.0 < w ≤ 36.0	Ж	5
36.0 < w ≤ 41.0	IIII	4

5

Number of emails	Tally	Frequency
15–20	IIII II	7
21–26	IIII IIII I	11
27–32	IIII II	7
33–38	III	3

2.6 Frequency polygons

1

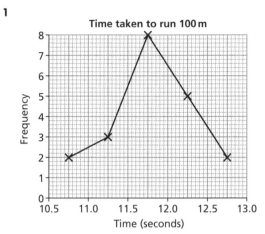

2

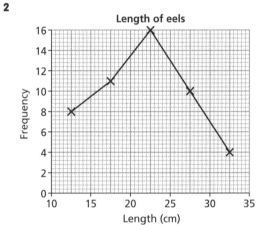

3 a

Speed (v miles per hour)	Tally	Frequency
$20 < v \leq 25$	II	2
$25 < v \leq 30$	III	3
$30 < v \leq 35$	III	3
$35 < v \leq 40$	IIII II	7
$40 < v \leq 45$	IIII III	8
$45 < v \leq 50$	IIII II	7

b

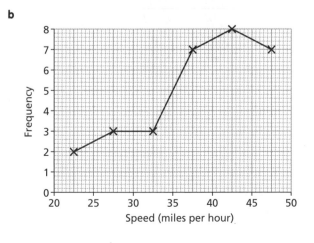

2.7 Cumulative frequency diagrams

1

Test score (t)	Frequency	Cumulative frequency
$20 < t \leq 30$	1	1
$30 < t \leq 40$	5	1 + 5 = 6
$40 < t \leq 50$	9	1 + 5 + 9 = 15
$50 < t \leq 60$	12	27
$60 < t \leq 70$	14	41
$70 < t \leq 80$	7	48
$80 < t \leq 90$	2	50

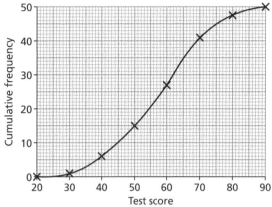

2

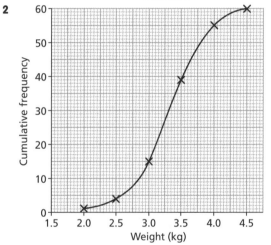

3

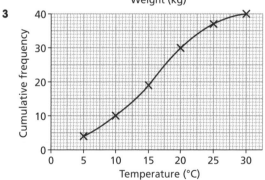

2.8 Box plots

1

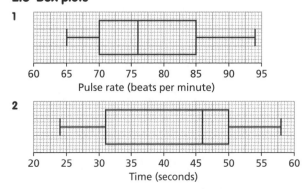

2

3

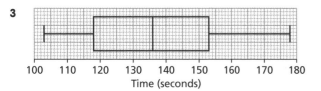

100   110   120   130   140   150   160   170   180
Time (seconds)

2.9 Histograms

1

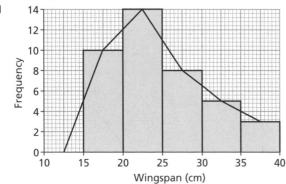

Wingspan (cm)

2

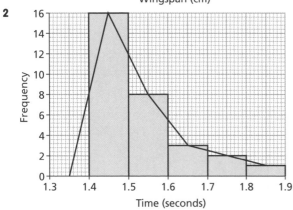

Time (seconds)

3

Height (h mm)	Tally	Frequency
$10 < h \leq 15$	ЖЖII	7
$15 < h \leq 20$	ЖЖ ЖЖI	11
$20 < h \leq 25$	ЖЖIIII	9
$25 < h \leq 30$	III	3

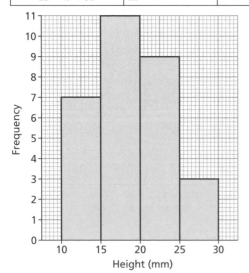

Height (mm)

2.10 Sample space diagrams

1

		\multicolumn{4}{c}{Red spinner}			
		1	2	3	4
Blue spinner	1	(1, 1)	(2, 1)	(3, 1)	(4, 1)
	2	(1, 2)	(2, 2)	(3, 2)	(4, 2)
	3	(1, 3)	(2, 3)	(3, 3)	(4, 3)
	4	(1, 4)	(2, 4)	(3, 4)	(4, 4)

2

		\multicolumn{6}{c}{Dice}					
		1	2	3	4	5	6
Coin	H	(1, H)	(2, H)	(3, H)	(4, H)	(5, H)	(6, H)
	T	(1, T)	(2, T)	(3, T)	(4, T)	(5, T)	(6, T)

3 a

		\multicolumn{6}{c}{Dice}					
		1	2	3	4	5	6
Spinner	1	2	3	4	5	6	7
	2	3	4	5	6	7	8
	3	4	5	6	7	8	9
	4	5	6	7	8	9	10

b   14

4

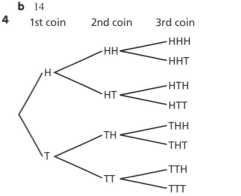

1st coin   2nd coin   3rd coin

2.11 Misleading diagrams

1   1   The vertical axis shows one value but there is no scale.
  2   The horizontal axis isn't labelled clearly.
2   Yes. The vertical scale doesn't start from zero so the increase in sales appears exaggerated.
3   1   The line is too thick.
  2   The horizontal axis is not uniform.
4   1   There is no vertical scale.
  2   The 3D effect makes it difficult to compare the heights of the bars.

Don't forget!

*   key
*   total; columns
*   time series
*   patterns
*   class intervals
*   frequency
*   class
*   lower quartile; maximum value
*   gaps
*   outcomes

Exam-style questions

1

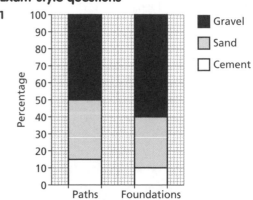

2

	Junior	Adult	Senior	Total
Standard	28	26	21	75
Full	3	29	14	46
Premium	1	27	11	39
Total	32	82	46	160

3

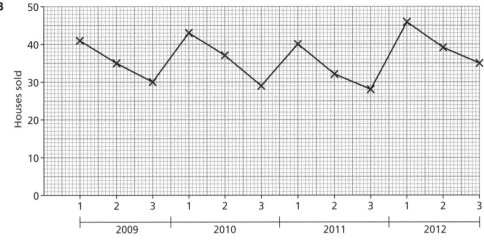

4

12	3 6 6
13	2 4 4 5 5 7
14	3 5 7 8
15	4 7 8 8 8 8 9 9
16	4 5

Key: 14 | 7
represents 147 rainy
days

5 a

Weight (*w* grams)	Tally	Frequency
$180 < w \leq 190$	卌 卌	10
$190 < w \leq 200$	卌 III	8
$200 < w \leq 210$	卌	5
$210 < w \leq 220$	II	2
$220 < w \leq 230$	II	2
$230 < w \leq 240$	III	3

b, c

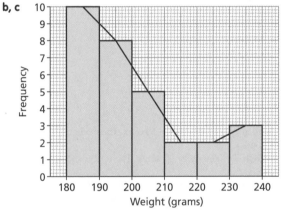

6

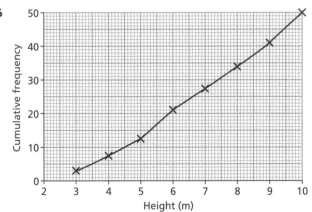

7

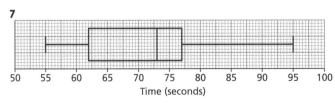

8 a

		Red spinner			
		1	**2**	**3**	**4**
Blue spinner	**1**	0	1	2	3
	2	1	0	1	2
	3	2	1	0	1
	4	3	2	1	0

b 4

9 1 The vertical scale doesn't start at 0.
  2 The 3D effect makes it difficult to compare the heights of the bars.
  3 The vertical axis shows numbers but no scale.

3 Calculating with data

3.1 Calculate means for grouped and ungrouped data

1 Total $= 3 + 0 + 2 + 1 + 5 + 2 + 1 + 2 = 16$
  Mean $= 16 \div 8 = 2$

2 Mean $= 4.3$ (1 d.p.)

3 Mean $= 23.7$ (1 d.p.)

4

Number of people in caravan (*p*)	Number of caravans (*f*)	$f \times p$
1	3	3
2	5	10
3	8	24
4	6	24
5	2	10
Total	24	71

Total number of people $= 3 + 10 + 24 + 24 + 10 = 71$
Total number of caravans $= 3 + 5 + 8 + 6 + 2 = 24$
Mean $= 71 \div 24 = 3.0$ (1 d.p.)

5 Mean $= 8.3$ (1 d.p.)

6 Mean $= 2.15$

7

Distance (*d*)	Frequency (*f*)	Mid-point (*x*)	$f \times x$
$5 < d \leq 10$	5	7.5	37.5
$10 < d \leq 15$	8	12.5	100
$15 < d \leq 20$	9	17.5	157.5
$20 < d \leq 25$	6	22.5	135
$25 < d \leq 30$	2	27.5	55
Total	30		485

Estimate of total distance $= 37.5 + 100 + 157.5 + 135 + 55$
  $= 485$ metres
Estimate of mean $= 485 \div 30 = 16.2$ metres (1 d.p.)

8 Estimate of mean $= 21\,°C$

9 Mean $= 36.5$ minutes

3.2 The median and interquartile range

1 The median is 5
  The position of the lower quartile Q1 is $\frac{(11 + 1)}{4} = 3$, Q1 $= 3$

  The position of the upper quartile Q3 is $3\frac{(11 + 1)}{4} = 9$, Q3 $= 8$

  The interquartile range IQR $= 5$

2 Median = 19, Lower quartile = 16, Upper quartile = 22,
Interquartile range = 6

3 Interquartile range = 6 cm

4 **a** Median = 173 cm
b Lower quartile = 166 cm
c Upper quartile = 179 cm
d Interquartile range = 13 cm

5 **a** Median = 3.35 kg
b Lower quartile = 3.0 kg
c Upper quartile = 3.6 kg
d Interquartile range = 0.6 kg

6 **a** Median = 15.5 °C
b Interquartile range = 10 °C

3.3 Moving averages and fixed-base index numbers

1 **a** $86 + 105 + 16 + 18 = 225$ $225 \div 4 = 56.25$
$105 + 16 + 18 + 45 = 184$ $184 \div 4 = 46$
$16 + 18 + 45 + 56 = 135$ $135 \div 4 = 33.75$
$18 + 45 + 56 + 15 = 134$ $134 \div 4 = 33.5$
The moving averages are 57.5, 56.25, 46, 33.75, 33.5

b There is a downward trend.

2 **a** 158.3, 164.7, 166, 167.7, 170, 174.3
b There is an upward trend.

3 **a** 90.5, 96.75
b There is an upward trend.

4 The total of Jack's scores is $10 \times 2 = 20$
The total of Bella's scores is $15 \times 3 = 45$
The combined total of both their scores is $20 + 45 = 65$
The total number of throws for both Jack and Bella is $10 + 15 = 25$
The combined mean $= \dfrac{\text{Combined total score}}{\text{Total number of throws}} = \dfrac{65}{25} = 2.6$

5 Mean = 60.8

6 Mean = £683.20

7 For 2013 the index number is $\dfrac{998}{876} \times 100 = 113.9$ (1 d.p.)

8 Index number = 102.1 (1 d.p.)

9 Index number = 109.1 (1 d.p)

3.4 Mean and standard deviation

1 Standard deviation $= \sqrt{231.5 - 15^2} = 2.5$ (1 d.p.)

2 Mean $= \dfrac{\Sigma x}{n} = \dfrac{84}{12} = 7$

$\dfrac{\Sigma x^2}{n} = \dfrac{680}{12} = 56.7$

Standard deviation $= \sqrt{56.7 - 7^2} = 2.8$ (1 d.p.)

3 Mean = 24.6, Standard deviation = 3.1 (1 d.p.)

4 **a** Mean = 11
b Standard deviation = 5.4 (1 d.p.)

5 **a** Mean = 29
b Standard deviation = 5.2 (1 d.p.)

6 **a** Mean = 25
b Standard deviation = 13.1 (1 d.p.)

Don't forget!

* divided
* frequency; frequencies
* mid-interval; sum; sum
* estimate
* quarter; $\dfrac{(n + 1)}{4}$; $\dfrac{(n + 1)}{2}$
* class interval; cumulative frequency
* spread
* trend
* time; base
* $\sqrt{\dfrac{\Sigma x^2}{n} - \bar{x}^2}$

Exam-style questions

1 Mean = 3.65 (3 s.f.)

2 Estimated mean = 24.1

3 Median = 148 grams, Interquartile range = 31 grams

4 $20 < t \leqslant 40$

5 **a** £19   **b** £5

6 **a** 25, 24.5
b There is an upward trend.

7 20 runs

8 Index number = 108.8 (1 d.p.)

9 **a** Mean = 41
b Standard deviation = 20.075 (3 d.p.)

4 Interpreting data

4.1 Interpret and compare charts and diagrams

1 **a** Chocolate
b Vanilla
c The section for coffee has 4 vertical squares.
Each square represents 2%
So the percentage that selected coffee is $4 \times 2\% = 8\%$
d 30%

2 **a** There are 8 intervals representing red squirrels in 1965
There are 18 intervals representing all of the squirrels in 1965
The fractions of the squirrels in 1965 that were red squirrels
is $\dfrac{8}{18} = \dfrac{4}{9}$

b $\dfrac{1}{41}$

3 **a** Week 3
b 19 girls
c 17 boys
d Week 3

4 **a** Normal/underweight
b Obese
c Many more Americans were heavier than normal in 2012 compared with 1962.

5 1 10 Y11 students took less than 14 seconds but only 4 Y7 students took less than 14 seconds.
2 9 Y7 students took more than 16 seconds but only 4 Y11 students took more than 16 seconds.

6 1 11 people scored less than 40% on Paper 2 but only 5 people scored less than 40% on Paper 1.
2 14 people scored more than 60% on Paper 1 but only 7 people scored more than 60% on Paper 2.

7 1 The temperature was below 24 °C on 11 days at Resort 2 but for only 3 days at Resort 1.
2 The temperature was above 26 °C for 19 days at Resort 1 but for only 10 days at Resort 2.

8 about £1400

9 about 63 marks

10 about £11 000

11 **a** 22 trees
b 13 trees

12 **a** 7 matches
b 12 matches

13 **a** 37 students
b 46 marks

14 **a** 13 minutes
b 6.5 minutes

15 The median for January is 3.5 hours. The median for December is 13 hours.
The IQR for January is 3.5 hours. The IQR for December is 5 hours.
The median for December is much higher than the median for January. The IQR is also greater in December than January.

16 **a** 4.3 hours
b 1.9 hours

17 The median for London is 31 whereas the median for the rest of England is 40 years.
The IQR for London is 27 whereas the IQR for the rest of England is 35 years.
The rest of England has the higher median age and the higher IQR.

18 **a** 76 miles
b 35 miles

19 The median for London is 51 mm whereas the median for Milan is 73 mm.
The IQR for London is 11 mm whereas the IQR for Milan is 14 mm.
The median for Milan is much higher than the median for London. Milan also has a slightly larger IQR.

20

Time (t minutes)	Frequency
$70 < t \leqslant 90$	5
$90 < t \leqslant 110$	8
$110 < t \leqslant 130$	10
$130 < t \leqslant 150$	4
$150 < t \leqslant 170$	2

21

Score (s)	Frequency
$30 < s \leqslant 60$	4
$60 < s \leqslant 90$	5
$90 < s \leqslant 120$	10
$120 < s \leqslant 150$	8
$150 < s \leqslant 180$	3

22

Height (h mm)	Frequency
$1.00 < h \leqslant 1.15$	3
$1.15 < h \leqslant 1.30$	7
$1.30 < h \leqslant 1.45$	9
$1.45 < h \leqslant 1.60$	10
$1.60 < h \leqslant 1.75$	6

23 a 16
  b 4
  c 6
24 a 20
  b 4
  c 5
25 a 12
  b 3

4.2 The modal class interval

1 $6 < h \leqslant 8$
2 $20 < l \leqslant 25$
3 $11.5 < t \leqslant 12.0$

4.3 Class intervals containing the median

1 $45 < t \leqslant 50$
2 $30 < w \leqslant 32$
3 $20 < d \leqslant 25$

4.4 Outliers

1 4 and 109
2

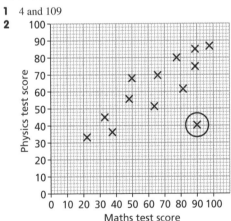

3 21 and 19
4

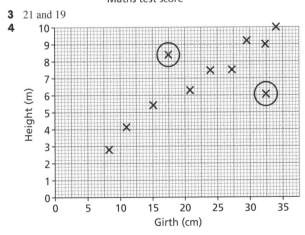

4.5 Lines of best fit and trend lines

1 Graph C
2 a Negative correlation
  b Graph B

3 a, b

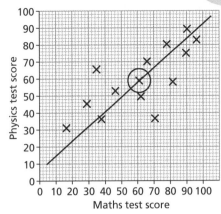

  c Positive correlation

4 a

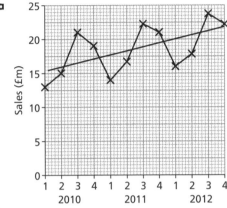

  b Upward trend

4.6 Skew

1 Positive skew
2 Negative skew
3 Positive skew

4.7 Comparing data – interquartile range, skew and standard deviation

1 $\Sigma x = 48 + 51 + 67 + 60 + 48 + 55 + 72 + 49 + 56 + 33 = 539$
  $\bar{x} = 539 \div 10 = 53.9$
  $\Sigma x^2 = 48^2 + 51^2 + 67^2 + 60^2 + 48^2 + 55^2 + 72^2 + 49^2 + 56^2 + 33^2$
  $= 30\,133$
  Standard deviation $= \sqrt{\dfrac{\Sigma x^2}{n} - \bar{x}^2} = \sqrt{\dfrac{30\,133}{10} - 53.9^2} = 10.397$ (3 d.p.)
2 The data for January has a slight positive skew.
  The data for December has a negative skew.
3 Mean for Labrador puppies is 5.54 kg.
  Standard deviation for Labrador puppies is $\sqrt{\dfrac{311.46}{10} - 5.54^2} = 0.674$
  The Labrador puppies have a higher mean but a very similar standard deviation compared with the Golden Retrievers.
4 a The skew of the data for London is slightly negative. The skew of the data for Milan is positive.
  b The interquartile range for the London data is 11. The interquartile range for the Milan data is 14.
5 Mean at start $= \dfrac{84.2}{8} = 10.525$, mean mid-way $= \dfrac{81.8}{8} = 10.225$
  Standard deviation at start $= 0.987$,
  standard deviation mid-way $= 0.109$
  The mean time has reduced by the mid-point of the season and the standard deviation has also reduced.

4.8 Making predictions

1 £7.9 million
2 26 000
3 a Third quarter
  b 96 pairs

4.9 Moving averages and fixed-base index numbers

1 a The fourth moving average is $\dfrac{(496 + 983 + 1496 + 1539)}{4} =$
  1128.5
  The moving averages are 1070.75, 1085.5, 1078, 1128.5, 1132.25
  b There is an upward trend.

2 a 344.5, 343.5
b There is a downward trend.
3 a 414, 425.25
b There is an upward trend.
4 The cost of diesel in January 2013 is 109.1% of its cost in January 2012. This represents a 9.1% increase.
5 Index number = 91.4
6 a 8.4% increase
b Index number = 117.9 (1 d.p.)

Don't forget!

* frequency
* median
* pattern
* line of best fit
* same
* correlation
* trend line
* symmetrically
* negative
* positive
* short-term
* upward
* downward
* flat
* percentage

Exam-style questions

1

Year	Peak	Off-peak	Flexi
2012	38%	46%	16%
2013	28%	44%	28%

2 1 14 Y7 students have a height of 1.5 m or less.
Only 7 Y11 students have a height of 1.5 m or less.
2 11 Y11 students have a height of 1.7 m or more.
Only 5 Y7 students have a height of 1.7 m or more.

3 a, c

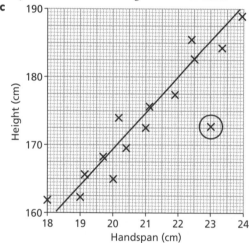

b about 177 cm
4 a 32 seconds
b 16 seconds
5 a 52 seconds
b 15 seconds
c Positive skew
6 a The median of the first group is 67. The median of the second group is 68, so the median of the second group is slightly higher than the first group.
b The IQR of the first group is 20. The IQR of the second group is 22. The IQR of the second group is higher than the IQR of the first group.

7 a

		Dice				
		1	**2**	**3**	**4**	**5**	**6**
4-sided spinner	**1**	2	3	4	5	6	7
	2	3	4	5	6	7	8
	3	4	5	6	7	8	9
	4	5	6	7	8	9	10

b 24
c 14

8 $\bar{x} = \frac{528}{10} = 52.8$
Standard deviation $= \sqrt{\frac{28\,466}{10} - 52.8^2} = 7.7$ (1 d.p.)
The second paper has a higher mean and a higher standard deviation.

9 a

Distance (d m)	Frequency
$2.5 < d \leqslant 3.0$	6
$3.0 < d \leqslant 3.5$	9
$3.5 < d \leqslant 4.0$	10
$4.0 < d \leqslant 4.5$	4
$4.5 < d \leqslant 5.0$	2

b $3.5 < d \leqslant 4.0$
c $3.5 < d \leqslant 4.0$
10 a 160.75, 153.25
b There is a downward trend.
11 a 6.7% increase
b Index number = 103.5 (1 d.p.)

5 Probability

5.1 Compare probability and relative frequency

1 a There are 5 possible outcomes.
2 of the outcomes are even.
Probability of even score $= \frac{2}{5} = 0.4$
b $\frac{7}{20} = \frac{35}{100} = 0.35$
c $\frac{21}{50} = \frac{42}{100} = 0.42$
d The answer to part **c** is based on more trials than the answer to part **b** and is closer to the theoretical value given in part **a**.
2 a 0.2
b 20 red counters
3 a $\frac{2}{24} = \frac{1}{12}$
b $\frac{6}{24} = \frac{1}{4}$
c Yes, the relative frequency of scoring 4 is much higher than the relative frequency of scoring 5.
d Conduct more trials.
4 a $\frac{1}{12}$
b $\frac{1}{4}$
c The values are quite different but the number of trials is very small so this is not unexpected.

5.2 Add probabilities

1 $1 - (0.28 + 0.35) = 0.37$
2 $\frac{4}{9}$
3 a 24% **b** 4 **c** 39% **d** 92%
4 0.36
5 a $\frac{7}{11}$ **b** $\frac{8}{11}$
6 a 21% **b** 63%
7 a 0.15 **b** 0.7 **c** 0.55

5.3 Use sample space diagrams to calculate probabilities

1 a 5
b The number of 4s in the table = 3
The total number of outcomes = 16
The probability that the total score will be 4
$= \frac{\text{Number of 4s in the table}}{\text{Total number of outcomes}} = \frac{3}{16}$
c $\frac{10}{16} = \frac{5}{8}$
2 a $\frac{7}{20}$ **b** $\frac{9}{20}$
3 a

	A	**B**	**C**
1	(A, 1)	(B, 1)	(C, 1)
2	(A, 2)	(B, 2)	(C, 2)
3	(A, 3)	(B, 3)	(C, 3)

b $\frac{2}{9}$

5.4 Use probability to estimate outcomes

1 Probability of a score of $4 = \frac{1}{6}$

Expected number of 4s $= \frac{1}{6} \times 30 = 5$

2 a $\frac{63}{80} = 0.7875$

b $0.7875 \times 200 = 157.5$
158 seeds

3 a 0.6   **b** 42 cars

4 a $\frac{1}{4}$ **b** 15 times

5 a 20%   **b** 10 times

5.5 Multiply probabilities using tree diagrams

1 a First card   Second card

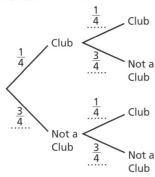

Each time: Probability of 'Not a Club' $= 1 - \frac{1}{4} = \frac{3}{4}$

b $\frac{3}{4} \times \frac{3}{4} = \frac{9}{16}$

2 a

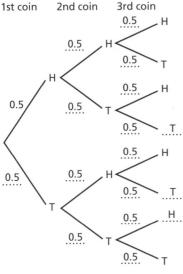

b 0.125

3 a First exam   Second exam

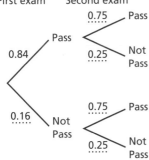

b 0.63

Don't forget!

* same
* the event; total
* estimated
* event occurred; trials
* increased
* the same time
* 1; 100%
* $1 - p$
* outcomes
* different
* the number of trials
* successive
* 1 or 100%
* multiply

Exam-style questions

1 a 0.66
b 0.7
2 a 5%
b 83%
c 11 times

3 a

	2	4	6
1	3	5	7
3	5	7	9
5	7	9	11

b $\frac{2}{9}$

c $\frac{8}{9}$

d 40 times

4 a First throw   Second throw

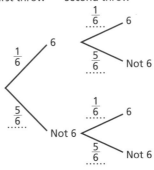

b $\frac{25}{36}$

Practice Paper

1

Variable	Type of data
Speed of a car	Continuous
Shoe size	Discrete
The number of teachers in a school	Discrete
The make of a computer	Categorical

2 a

Calories (x)	Tally	Frequency
$900 < x \leq 1000$	ЖІІ	7
$1000 < x \leq 1100$	Ж	5
$1100 < x \leq 1200$	ЖІІ	7
$1200 < x \leq 1300$	ЖІІІ	8
$1300 < x \leq 1400$	ІІІ	3

b $1200 < x \leq 1300$
c $1100 < x \leq 1200$

3 a A possible question is:
What are your views on the proposal to build some new houses on part of the town centre car park?
☐ In favour
☐ Not in favour
☐ No strong opinion
Make sure that you:
* present the question clearly and without bias
* allow for each possible response.

b These shopkeepers are a biased sample of the population since the proposed development will affect them directly.

4 a

First spin   Second spin

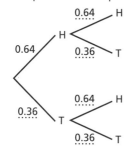

b 0.4096

5 a

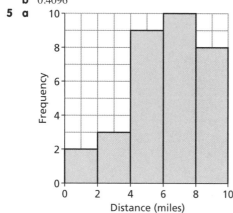

b The skew is negative.

c 6.2 miles (1 d.p.)

d $\dfrac{9}{16}$

6 a

1	5							
2	3	6	6	7	7			
3	3	4	5	7	7	7	9	9
4	0	2	2	2	3	6	8	8
5	0	2	2	4	8			

Key: 2 | 3
represents 2.3 kg

b 3.9 kg

c 1.5 kg

d

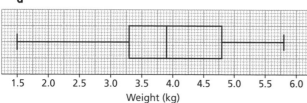

7 a 0.3

b 12 times

8 a 108.2 (1 d.p.)

b 8.2% increase

9 59.7 (1 d.p.)

10 a

		First spin		
		R	**W**	**B**
	R	(R, R)	(W, R)	(B, R)
Second spin	**W**	(R, W)	(W, W)	(B, W)
	B	(R, B)	(W, B)	(B, B)

b $\dfrac{1}{9}$

c $\dfrac{6}{9} = \dfrac{2}{3}$

11 Median for South is 20 minutes.
Interquartile range for South is 3 minutes.
The times for vehicles travelling South have a lower median and a lower interquartile range.

12 14

13 Some possible answers are:
It is quicker/cheaper than taking a census.

14 a, b

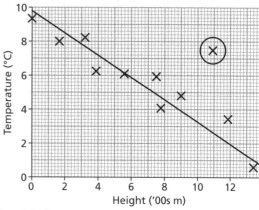

c about 3.2 °C

d There is a strong negative correlation between height and temperature.

15 a 277, 278

b There is an upward trend.

16 a $\dfrac{2}{10} = 0.2$

b $\dfrac{1}{4} = 0.25$

c The answers are quite close considering that the number of trials is so small.

17 1 The 3D effect makes it difficult to read the bar heights.
2 The vertical scale doesn't start at 0.
3 The numbers on the vertical scale have no units.

18 1 The mode (4) is the same for both books.
2 Book A has more very short words.

19 a $\dfrac{9}{10}$

b $\dfrac{7}{10}$

20 a

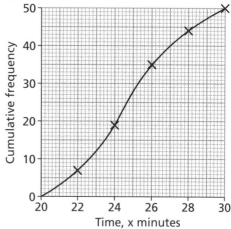

b about 22

21 about 47

22 a 3.12

b 1.395